Talking Your Way Up The Career Ladder

SPEAK UP & MOVE UP!

R. H. LEWIS

From *Speak Up and Move Up!*

*Leaders must inform persuade, advise, explain,
inspire, question, sell, challenge, and motivate.
They must be able to do so in writing or orally
or in combination. The leader or manager
skillful in both areas, assuming substance
and style, will make it big time!*

About the Author

President of Aurora, IL Toastmasters Club

Instructor of parliamentary procedure for Chicago Jaycees

Instructor of Dale Carnegie Courses

Chaired state speakers bureau for Taxpayers Federation of Illinois

Shared speakers platform at Washington D. C. convention
with then Senator JFK

Interviewed congressmen for public television

Had radio program in Spokane, WA—"Political thought for the day"

Spokane city councilman and state senator

Professional motivational speaker and management consultant

INTRODUCTION

"TELL THEM what you're going to tell 'em...tell them...then tell them what you told 'em." That coaching is offered in Toastmasters.

"Act the way you want to be and soon you'll be the way you act." That equally memorable line is offered to those who take the basic course offered by Dale Carnegie & Associates. In addition, the "Speak Up, Jaycees" program has helped many young men grow in their determination to become leaders.

In this work an attempt will be offered to stimulate readers to turn their career ladders into extension ladders. As we achieve specific objectives we set even higher goals. Organizations write mission statements. Boards conduct strategic planning sessions. Businesses for profit and those in non-profit endeavors have known policy statements. Printed goals and objectives should be known to everyone involved in an organization's existence and purpose.

If a business plan is of value to those aiming to make a profit, doesn't it make sense for an individual to have a personal development plan to enhance career growth?

Dreaming of one's ultimate career-desire is fun. The challenge is to engineer that dream into reality. This work is designed to stimulate, illustrate, and even guide efforts toward fulfillment of your career dream!

ONE

Becoming a Better Communicator

> *"Of all the talents bestowed upon men, none is so precious as the gift of oratory. He who enjoys it wields a power more durable than that of a great king. He is an independent force in the world."*
>
> WINSTON CHURCHILL

"WE HAVE NOTHING TO FEAR BUT FEAR ITSELF!" That memorable one-liner was uttered by a man in a wheelchair, a victim of polio. President Franklin Delano Roosevelt's fireside chats via radio demonstrated the power of the spoken word during trying times—the Great Depression in the 1930s and World War II in the 1940s.

Jesus Christ never wrote a book or a manifesto. He spoke to the world of the moment and continues to communicate to every succeeding generation. How influential was his oral message? Today it is considered gospel by over 2.15 billion professing Christians. That message is based on forgiveness, love, and respect for others. (The second largest group of religious practitioners is Islam, estimated at over 1.2 billion practitioners.)

Martin Luther King, Jr. advocated peaceful demonstration in

his pursuit of equal treatment of the races. His "I Have a Dream" speech made a dramatic social impact.

FDR and MLK required no further identification while they were alive or even for many of us today. True, they both had detractors, but FDR was the only president elected to a third term (and then an uncompleted fourth). MLK stirred the passions of his audiences. Even his critics give him that. Did he make an impact? How many individuals have a holiday in their name? There's Christmas and Columbus and St. Patrick's Day. Washington's and Lincoln's birthdays are now consolidated into Presidents Day.

Ronald Reagan was dubbed "The Great Communicator." His speeches were straightforward and exhibited substance and style, the two principal ingredients of speeches by professional or merely competent performers. Reagan charmed audiences. Charm has been defined as "the ability to make your listener think that both of you are pretty wonderful."

With his background as a sportscaster and an actor, Ronald Reagan had a sense of timing above and beyond his speechmaking. His persuasive powers had a lot to do with America winning the Cold War with the Soviet Union.

The point is this: The ability to speak to a group is essential if one is to be a leader, be it in a corporate setting, trade union, political life, civic activity, church, or in non-profit or volunteer work or efforts.

Possibly the most appreciated speech as a commencement address was delivered by President Harry S. Truman on June 9, 1950. A hard rain was pelting the University of Missouri graduating class, which included many WWII veterans. Dignitaries were at mid-field in the football stadium, sheltered by a pagoda.

Presidents in earlier years had to listen to lengthy flowery introductions designed to curry favor. Congress in its wisdom (that is not sarcasm, as is too often the case when that phrase is used) passed legislation providing the only introduction to be utilized is "Ladies and Gentlemen, the President of the United States."

HST rose, smiled, and said, "No one wants to hear a speech on a day like this. Good luck to you all!" Cheers drowned out the occasional thunder.

If nominations were made for the best short speech, a contender would be the answer General Anthony McAuliffe gave to the German demand for surrender of the 501st paratroopers encircled in Bastogne, Belgium. His answer: "Nuts!"

FDR's words about having nothing to fear but fear itself might well be directed to an audience of entrepreneurs and business executives who, despite many lofty achievements, respond in surveys that their greatest fear is to be called upon to speak to a group at a meeting or function. Especially one that will be reported by the media. Elbert Hubbard's quote comes to mind: "The greatest mistake in life is to go through life fearing to make a mistake."

A national survey revealed that the five most feared activities are the following:

Going to the dentist, preparing taxes, public speaking, cleaning house, and job interviews. If such a survey had been restricted to executives, it was intimated, the sequence would have had public speaking at the top of the list.

Leaders must inform, persuade, advise, explain, inspire, question, sell, challenge, and motivate. They must be able to do so in writing or orally or in combination. The leader or manager skillful in both areas, assuming substance and style, *will* make it big-time!

Any adult blessed with normal faculties can talk. Talking effectively for personal and career growth and income enhancement is another matter.

Sometimes a person may tell a lie by remaining silent. To question or challenge a statement or the direction of a group or a leader or a manager sometimes requires courage. Even church deacons, Girl Scout mothers, and stalwarts of the community have sat mute, possibly feeling they must be mentally out of step with the majority. Such silence is usually interpreted as agreement. Muttering "I wish I had spoken up" often comes too late, maybe even in bed near midnight. It takes courage to speak up, to dissent, or even just to question a person in a superior position. It is difficult for some to disagree agreeably.

Courage cannot be communicated through the pages of this work, but one can experience improved skill in asserting one's position by determining to become a better speaker.

Speaking conversationally in, to, or with small groups is not too much of a challenge for most. Most people who graduate to "the platform" find the experience exhilarating, exciting, personally fulfilling—and often profitable!

You can be at any stage of your career and decide you want to develop or improve your speaking ability. Opportunities may simply occur or they may be created. Some might even be "grasped," if subtlety is exercised appropriately. Program chairpersons are always in need, if not immediately then sometime in the future. Americans attend many meetings ritually on a given schedule. Service clubs, women's organizations, and business meetings, conferences, and conventions present opportunities for one to tell his or her story and show talent in so doing.

Existing opportunities may be dependent upon one's present level of sophistication, position in the world of commerce, and/or civic/social experiences of potential interest. These factors will influence the direction one will take in pursuit of opportunities. For example, one may be involved in sales meetings, training sessions, or the Christmas party committee. One may present awards for a safety record or bowling tournament, or simply participate in staff meetings. Are there first aid classes to be taught, high school or career day tours to be conducted? Is someone taking the message of your organization into the school system at appropriate high school or college level? If not, perhaps "someone" could volunteer.

If one reports to a board of directors or to stockholders, doing better could pay dividends.

Conference and convention speakers enjoy travel, honoraria, and career enhancement, recognition in the form of higher income, and personal satisfaction.

Public speaking is the route taken by some who wish to grow from being a manager to being a leader. *Leaders do the right things or see to it that the right things are being done, striving for effect and results.* They are concerned primarily with the "what" and "why." They delegate authority and responsibility to managers, people they are confident are in the right niches and can be motivated to maximize their talents. (There is one talent that exceeds all others. The greatest talent is the ability to recognize, inspire, and utilize talents of others—while helping them grow!)

Leaders employ managers, vital to the accomplishment of understood and agreed-upon objectives, conscious of and adhering to the organization's written mission statement. *Managers do things right or see to it that things are being done right, efficiently, and for results.* They are keenly aware of the "what" and "why," but more intimately involved in the "how," the "who," and the "when."

Leaders deal more with policy, managers with procedures. But—in many instances there is a dual role being played. Many managers double as leaders, being first to initiate and sell to superiors the "right things" and then seeing to it that things are done right.

Leaders are not "natural born." They have to develop, cultivate, and nurture their skills to maximize the talents they may have. Work and dedication are imperative. Competent speakers do not spring from the forehead of Zeus. A speaker, unless it is the boss, has little more than a minute to "hook" the listener, who makes an early judgment about how much attention the subject and speaker merit. Readers of business memos, letters, or manuals may plow through even the dullest material. Readers of books or magazine articles may stay with written material for a few pages or even a chapter to determine interest and value.

Some leaders make it solely on their technical skills. Community leaders, however, from whatever fields of endeavor, are the ones most likely to be quoted in the media. Again, substance must be there, as style without substance is afforded only to comedians.

Illustrations make a point. Golfers may use the following example (bowlers or tennis players will have to adapt):

The wife of a friend couldn't understand how anyone could find enjoyment in "...chasing a little white ball around a field, putting it into a hole, and then repeating and repeating the process."

When their children were grown she decided she would not be a golf widow. She tried it and, predictably, got hooked.

One doesn't have to be good to enjoy golf or bowling, for example, but getting better is fun in every endeavor. There is satisfaction, even a thrill, sometimes, in improving. So it is with public speaking, which simply means talking to more than a few people outside the home.

A formal course is one route to take. More ("good stuff") will be said later of Toastmasters, opportunities in the U.S. Junior Chamber of Commerce (Jaycees), adult evening courses at a (nearby?) college, and the Dale Carnegie Management Course, which merits credit for my portrayal above of the role of leaders and managers.

When Emil Ludwig wrote of Napoleon's Italian campaign, he noted: "Half of what he achieves is achieved by the power of words." The emotion, the depth, and sincerity of one's feelings are felt by an audience. Audiences are receptive to a sincere compliment but can readily spot insincere flattery. Honest praise is especially valuable when a speaker has some tough recommendations to offer.

Emotion can be an effective tool. When one speaks or writes, words should be chosen tastefully. On rare occasions they may have to be eaten.

Andy Rooney, the well-known wordsmith and sometimes cynic on *60 Minutes*, a syndicated columnist and a literary humorist, wrote, "I can't figure out whether the average convention is an honest business meeting or a boondoggle wrapped as a Christmas present the executives give to themselves once a year."

One opportunity enjoyed at conventions is to make a suggestion. There is risk or reward involved, as one offering a suggestion is likely to be made chairperson of the appropriate committee. That, of course, means that person will be obliged to attend the organization's convention next year. If one likes the "Christmas present," opening one's mouth is a way to get on the road to becoming what some might call a professional conventioneer.

Self-examination is a starting point for making a determination about becoming a competent speaker and thus a leader. Here is a summary of the primary characteristics and qualities leaders are likely to share:

- ▶▶ The ability to recognize, employ, and nurture talent in others.

- ▶▶ The ability to lead or manage others—as a team-builder—to get desired results.

- ▶▶ Loyalty to and support of peers and those above and below their stations.

- ▶▶ Interviewing and hiring skills beneficial to applicants, employed or not, and thus to the employing organization.

- ▶▶ Skills that make performance evaluation sessions enjoyable and productive—and never a necessary evil for the executive or a traumatic experience for the individual whose performance is being discussed. (More later, of course.)

- ▶▶ Teaching, training, and coaching skills that encourage and develop potential to the utmost, even if it means a protégé moves not just upward but around some and possibly even outward in a career journey upward.

- ▶▶ A well-deserved good reputation at home as a parent and spouse, which is paramount, but also respect in the community, among peers in the broader field of endeavor, and probably even among competitors.

- ▶▶ A high tolerance level for mistakes made in efforts nobly motivated, with subscription to the admonition that "If a man is to be hung he should be so guilty that even his friends will come to the hanging."

- ▶▶ The ability to conduct meetings professionally, on the

prescribed time schedule, implementing an agenda with orderliness and fairness to all participants.

▶▶ The ability to motivate by communicating orally and in writing in a manner that is understandable and acceptable.

Now you add one characteristic or trait or talent, or more, of special significance to you.

You will find some of these points elaborated upon in this book. Successful marketers know the value of repetition. (Haven't you seen several commercials over and over.)

A speaker was asked, "How did you gain confidence on the platform?"

"Well," came the response, "the same way I learned to ride a bicycle. I just kept getting up until I got the hang of it."

That's one way to approach a challenge. Then there are those who look for a blueprint, a map, or counsel from those who've "been there, done that." Reading a golf magazine won't make one a professional, but there are valuable tips there.

Reading *Speak Up and Move Up!* won't make one a brilliant conversationalist, a great orator, or president of an organization, but here's what it *will* do:

▶▶ It will stimulate one's thinking.

▶▶ It should motivate the reader to do something.

▶▶ It just might enhance career growth,

▶▶ It really could change one's life!

Once half-mastered, platform performance is fun! Those who dream really big might think of the honoraria bestowed upon big-name speakers. Television anchors get twenty-five thousand or more. Former presidents and vice presidents may be given as much as two hundred thousand—former president Bill Clinton, for example. (Some might suspect this is a "gift." It was at a time when he had huge legal bills to pay.) His income for appearances during the two years following his leaving office amounted to almost ten million dollars, all perfectly legal.

Al Gore, former vice president, has become a successful author and an "authority" on global warming. Speaking appearances contribute to his net worth, now in the tens of millions of dollars.

This is the extreme, of course. Speakers and writers often use extremes when citing examples, and these obviously are not typical or realistic for speakers who have not been in such high offices. However, leaders of non-profit causes or movements, nationally known executives, and celebrities can and do command big bucks for appearances. Those conducting motivational or sales seminars and published authors do quite well. Attendees or their sponsoring organizations pay healthy fees in hopes of enhancement of careers. Speakers' fees will not be the primary source of income for most managers or leaders, but those who communicate effectively can expect to move up their career ladders, elevate personal prestige, and merit higher incomes.

Entrepreneurs raising venture capital persuade prospective investors to risk their dollars. Many fund-raisers start in that field after attending seminars or forums at which speech instructors and marketing experts coached them on how to make an effective pitch.

Witnesses called upon to testify in court or to give depositions are usually coached in advance by attorneys and maybe even specialists. Included in such preparation is the counsel to "Say the least possible."

Talk is not cheap when it helps determine the outcome of what may be a lawsuit involving large sums of money. Knowing when to shut up is a talent.

An example: An expert witness in a hundred-million-dollar lawsuit offered a whiz-bang summarizing comment during a deposition. It prompted the opposing lawyer to whisper to him on the elevator ride as they departed the building, "I sure wish you were on our side."

The observation offered was, "The regulators were in a tough spot, as it is well-known the chief offender (president of a large financial institution) has been the biggest contributor and chief supporter of the governor. I do not believe the regulators were naïve, but they were understandably intimidated—and gutless."

That statement prompted an out-of-court settlement for five million. The expert witness objected, "Why offer five million? I wouldn't pay them one cent."

"Court costs would be that much," came the answer. "Look at what we have to pay you—and others—to do all that reading and research and travel, plus our lawyers, who don't come for peanuts, and this would drag on for weeks or months."

One person's oral paragraph had a ninety-five million dollar impact. His fee for hours of reading, traveling a long distance twice, and his expertise as a witness resulted in a new Lincoln Town Car. No wonder court costs are so high.

Your ability to speak well is not likely to lead you into such a dramatic event, but your decision and determination to be a better conversationalist and a competent platform performer will have an impact on your career.

So—do you really believe that just doing a good job will result in a significant salary increase and someday maybe advancement? That can happen, especially if one is performing better than any predecessor has done in the position.

One must stand out from the crowd to be noticed—and you know the competition is tough. Public speaking skills may provide an edge!

> *"A man can succeed at anything for which he has unlimited enthusiasm."*
>
> CHARLES SCHWAB

TWO

Are You Ready to Determine Your Direction?

> *"What knowledge is absorbed is never lost. It increases by its own power and provides the means to reach an end—all its attainments help to new conquests."*

DANIEL WEBSTER

NOW THAT WE ARE ACQUAINTED, let's talk in the first and second person. Your responses to four questions may help you organize a plan for career development. Take a few minutes to put your answers in writing and you'll surprise and challenge yourself. These are the key questions career counselors ask:

1. What and where do you wish to be ultimately? (Your lifetime goal.)

2. What and where are you determined to be ten years from today?

3. What and where are you planning to be one year from today?

4. What must you do, starting right now or no later than

tomorrow morning, to be what and where you want to be a year from today? The first three were relatively easy. The "doing" is the real challenge.

Assuming we are in agreement that personal growth is the general goal, developing your potential as a platform performer can have measurable benefits. You will have more positive feelings and thus confidence in the following:

- Standing up to have your say.
- Addressing small and ultimately large groups.
- Talking to your boss and others in superior levels of your organization.
- Talking comfortably—and beneficially and profitably—with subordinates.
- Nominating a qualified candidate to some office.
- Serving as a panelist.
- Speaking with few or no notes. (We'll deal with memory techniques later.)
- Debating without arguing—disagreeing in an agreeable manner.
- Chairing meetings, then conferences, and ultimately conventions.
- Being a master or mistress of ceremonies or the presiding officer.
- "Talking" more effectively in your writing.
- Contacting political office holders, maybe even lobbying.
- Motivating volunteers.
- Talking to and dealing with the media!
- Finally, having more fun in your work—at a higher income level.

Your goals will be extended as accomplishments are made to occur. As we grow, so do challenges and opportunities. Someone once wrote, "Goals are like rainbows. As we advance they recede." Those executing their climb up their individual career ladders find they are extension ladders!

Paradoxical as it may seem, there are highly paid executives who actually are shy. Dale Carnegie and Associates is a national franchise offering classes usually available in areas accessible to most interested parties. Decades ago Dale Carnegie wrote *How to Win friends and Influence People*. It was a best seller for years, third only behind the Bible and the Boy Scout Handbook. He originally taught at a local YMCA (Young Men's Christian Association), then developed a national network of franchises. Over the decades it became big business.

"Human Relations and Effective Speaking" was the original course. A sales course and a management course followed. It could prove worthwhile to explore what's available in your area that could be worked into your schedule. Exploring options costs nothing but your investment of a couple of hours.

Other options include a course or courses in the Adult Evening Division (or some equivalent name) of a local college. Business Communications or Advanced Speech, by whatever designation, could be part of initiating your long-range plan.

One size does not fit all, so your personal wants will dictate your actions. Nothing happens without commitment and action. Evaluation of your desires may help establish a direction.

I would prefer:

- Being in a smaller____or larger____organization or of no matter____.
- A more structured or organized atmosphere____.
- More freedom to do my own thing____.
- Less pressure and fewer deadlines____.

- More variety, fresh challenges equal to my skill and intellect_____.
- Assignments that have a stopping point instead of so much routine_____.
- More involvement in goal-setting_____.
- More opportunity to show my skill in writing_____.
- More use of my oral talents_____.
- More time alone_____.
- Less paperwork_____.
- More supervisory authority_____.
- To own my own business_____.

You may now have fresh insights about who and what you are and what changes you wish to consider. Visualize three situations: First, an in-house conversation in which you must consider a different position. You know or can determine what considerations would make a change attractive or less than appealing. We won't belabor that here, but are you ready for such a conversation?

Now the second visualization: An executive recruiter, sometimes called a "headhunter" and sometimes an "executive-pirate," approaches you. You may be assured your background has been researched. Probably discreetly, you have been checked out pretty well. Previous employers, if any, were asked if they would rehire. Your friends and former and maybe even current associates may have been queried, however subtly. Some may have been made aware of the reason for interest in you. Your academic background is known. The recruiter may ask if you have an up-to-date resume. Obviously, it is advisable and wise to always have one fairly current. The interested client may or may not be identified in initial conversations. If a geographical move is necessary, you may be sure you are on the short list of candidates if that information is revealed. A recruiter is likely to be friendly but will obviously want to be certain of a good fit for client and prospect.

Some form of conversation along these lines will occur: "Our research indicates that in previous and present employment you bring solutions, not just problems, to the table. You accept responsibility, your peers say, and do not try to shift blame to others. Also, and perhaps most important, you're a team-builder, helping others develop and maximize talents. And I assure you, it doesn't hurt that you can write a grammatically correct paragraph!"

There will be pauses, similar to those used by reporters and television interviewers of politicians, creating a vacuum to see if the interviewee feels obliged to fill it. That's when there is the greatest danger of foot-in-mouth disease. A smile of appreciation and a nod may be appropriate. Silence seldom is a problem unless one is permitting silence to be interpreted as agreement when a question or challenge would be the honest approach.

"Finally," the interviewer may continue if you offer satisfactory answers to pertinent questions, "we are impressed with your ability to conduct meaningful and productive meetings. You speak well from the platform. These are the key reasons my client probably will be making an offer I hope you will find difficult to refuse."

You may be sure the professional recruiter knows more about you than that, but doesn't want to go overboard in telling you how good you are. The salary may be negotiable. If you are being considered for a leadership position, that recruiter knows you are calm under fire, you do not buckle under stress, and even your carriage reflects confidence. Obviously, under the conditions described, you are in a strong bargaining position. An eager potential employer and an appropriately enthusiastic candidate leads to a win/win relationship.

It is possible one headhunter may be after a quick commission, while another may see your talent as something that will grow and thus could provide repeat business. We should not knock such self-interest or selfish motivation. After all, are we guiltless of wanting to make an honest buck? Style and substance vary, and there is no magic formula to determine the character of the person approaching you with an opportunity. Your gut feeling will probably be accurate.

Visualization number three: You are thinking of "up or out," but do not wish to be precipitous. Maybe you have contacts with a career counselor. If you are in an above-entry level position you may wish to consider professional guidance and/or help. Except for on-campus free counseling, not many in the early career stage retain such services or have friends in a recruiting firm. It is possible a high-level staffer might be available, trusted, and willing to offer some insight to a junior who illustrates ambition. Such counseling is an art, not a science.

Those prepared for potential change and challenges will be in control of an orderly process beneficial to one's self (and to the family?).

Emphasis in this work is on the development and nurturing of speaking ability, thus stimulating mental rehearsal for the day one of our three situations occurs. Some things we have to experience to gain skills and understanding. The cliché "practice makes perfect" is not valid if we are practicing incorrectly. Professional guidance can make practice worthwhile and valuable. "Be yourself" is well-intentioned advice, but not beneficial to an incompetent performer. You want to do and be better, to polish rough edges and to build strength.

There are those who hope Opportunity will knock on their door. Then there are those who knock on Opportunity's door!

Those who speak effectively when the door opens will be heard. The ability to speak well, persuasively, even passionately, is an attribute common to most, not all, leaders. The polishing of one's speaking ability has been a key factor in the attainment of many top spots. Open your mouth to make a suggestion, offer an idea, or state (politely) a criticism, and you can be thrust into a position of more responsibility for what is going to happen next. It may be a committee chair or election to an office. We've all either experienced that or at least observed such.

You want to polish existing attributes, develop new talents, and learn new skills. Being yourself isn't good enough. You want to be better than you are. Even if you're a CEO and have the world by the tail you haven't reached your potential. You have the opportunity to give more to others.

We are all on individual career ladders. Thus, those more experienced may have to gloss over points that seem obvious but could be new to others. Some readers may have started up or are starting up their ladder of life's adventures from such a disadvantaged set of circumstances that it was a struggle to reach the second-from-the-bottom rung. A privileged few are born into well-to-do families with stature and ready opportunity. Their challenge may be to not fall from or slip down their ladders. They usually want to prove themselves by climbing to an even higher rung.

Most of us start or started above the absolute bottom rung. Those climbing to leadership positions most often enhanced their qualifications via the educational process.

Attitude and aptitude can make or break us. Self-improvement is what the ambitious strive for. (Winston Churchill, when criticized for ending a sentence with a preposition, said, "That is arrant pedantry, up with which I will not put." He may have been the one who said, "It's my infinitive and I'll split it if I want to.")

Improvement in those around us is what leaders and managers strive for as well, but the wise ones start with self-improvement. That starts with an attitude.

Blessed are those who have this attitude:

▶▶ I need to improve.

▶▶ I want to improve.

▶▶ I can improve.

▶▶ I will improve!

Blessed are those with this aptitude:

▶▶ To master fundamentals in one's chosen area.

▶▶ To understand basic concepts of the program at hand.

▶▶ To counsel others that knowledge is not power unless put into action.

▶▶ To have the foresight and eagerness to look ahead.

What we like and where we are on our career ladders merits analysis. A personal profile may stimulate some new thoughts. The scoring of one to ten in the categories listed below should reveal if you are living up to the admonition "Know thyself." When you consider scores take a look at the one or two weakest areas of satisfaction, and ask yourself, "So what am I going to do about it?"

- Educational achievements_____
- Early career development_____
- Advancement chances_____
- Job satisfaction_____
- Personal relations with peers and subordinates_____
- Relationship with supervisors and superior offices_____
- My self-development program_____
- Control of my career progress_____
- My interest and enthusiasm level_____
- Opportunity for self-fulfillment_____
- My efforts—and chances—to get my boss promoted_____
- My commitment to excellence in my present position_____
- My ability to deal with changes or "the new"_____
- The perceptions of my peers about my abilities_____

What is a satisfactory score? That's up to the individual level of satisfaction. These ratings are simply thought stimulators. Pause and think. Your future is in your own hands. You are not at the mercy of anyone but yourself.

Luck may play a role in your success, but as one of your friends has said, it is likely that "The harder I work, the luckier I get."

> *"Keep away from people who try to belittle your ambitions. Small people always do that, but the really great make you feel that you, too, can become great."*
>
> MARK TWAIN

THREE

Is Your Position a Foundation, a Dead End, or a Springboard?

"The greatest works are those done by the ones. The hundred do not often do much—the companies never; it is the units—the single individuals, that are the power and the might. Individual effort is, after all, the grand thing."

UNKNOWN

LIFE IS A TRIP. We can drift and hope to get lucky or we can plan a direction toward a desirable destination. We may be detoured, stymied, or even blocked in various legs of the trip. We may have to resort to Plan B, a different direction to get to the same or maybe an altered destination. We do not always have complete control of our destinies, but actions under our control certainly play a significant role in what we make happen and thus to a large degree, what happens to us. Those waiting for their ships to come in are dreamers. Realists expect their ships to come because they have each launched a ship.

Let's face it: Leaders have to be egotistical—to varying degrees, to be sure. One must be, to stand before a group and espouse a point of view. Edward Hodnett, author of *Effective Presentations*, wrote, "You need to steer the thinking of your listeners or readers through three FIR steps—Facts, Inferences, Recommendations. Nailing down the inferences to be drawn from the facts you present is what persuades an audience that your recommendations are inevitable."

Rewards vary. Competence usually reaps monetary reward. To many there is an equal or greater reward: the respect of others and the satisfaction of "doing one's thing."

Here are the steps to get started on your Action Plan:

1. **EVALUATE YOUR PRESENT POSITION**

   Is my foundation also a springboard?

   Am I doing my present job better than anyone has ever done it?

   Do I present solutions rather than just problems to my superiors?

2. **REVIEW YOUR JOB DESCRIPTION**

   Is it results-oriented as opposed to being a laundry list of tasks?

   Do my boss and I agree as to what my job really entails? New duties may have been added, old ones discontinued. Would a successor and/or a new boss understand it by what is in writing?

   Rewrite it as it really is and get concurrence from your boss.

3. **ANALYZE YOUR INDUSTRY OR CAREER FIELD**

   Are there growth opportunities?

   What is the outlook for my particular area of expertise?

   Is there career mobility? Am I dead-ended behind someone or is there opportunity to move around? Could I take my skills and talent to another employer in the same or a related general field?

4. POLISH AND DEVELOP SKILLS

Am I really learning my trade, not just "tricks of the trade"?

Is there something I can do to add one skill to my resume?

What can I do to achieve "outside" recognition for my talents or contributions?

Can I establish myself as a recognized authority?

What specific steps can I take to improve my communications skills, oral and written? (This is an ongoing, not a "quickie" effort.)

5. PREPARE ACADEMICALLY

Is there an educational gap I should address?

Am I willing to undertake a realistic study program, incorporating formal courses, seminars, workshops, conferences, and even a correspondence course if necessary?

Do I have or can I develop a specialty to make me an authority?

Do I really know how to study effectively? (We'll discuss memory techniques, including acronyms, later.)

6. STRUCTURE YOUR READING PROGRAM

Am I willing to set up a reading schedule, i.e., a book a week—or?

Am I staying abreast of job-related reading of trade/ professional journals?

Could I broaden my leadership and/or management-oriented horizon by reading some basic or current germane books?

7. DEVELOP OTHERS

How soon can I review and upgrade (or develop?) my plan to help subordinates grow?

Am I paying maximum attention to my family relationships? An appreciated and supportive spouse enhances one's career growth.

Do I share with subordinates my philosophies of life and work. (You set the values and the tone of the workplace. Solicit input—listen!)

8. UPDATE YOUR RESUME

Am I in control of my career, ready to shift gears and walk away when I desire, or as might become necessary?

Is there a professional or a trusted associate to critique my resume?

Is it updated every six months—and always handy?

Is there evidence of outside recognition (news clippings) and published works I can show to an interviewer?

Look again at the one- and ten-year plan you developed. In light of the above exercise is there need for modification or elaboration? Do you have a schedule to measure your progress?

Write major strategies and tactics toward measurable results. Develop an informal Plan B based on "What if...?" Pre-planned options can turn roadblocks into negotiable detours.

Start by brainstorming with confidants, including your spouse, or you may choose to do so by yourself with a pen and notebook or on your computer. This is not a time to be tidy, neat, or orderly. Record ideas as they occur, with refining and organizing to come later.

The growth game is competitive. Time, effort, imagination, and work are necessary for those who wish to develop plans that will lead to outscoring the drifters. Leaders and managers are keenly interested in building a winning team. It all starts with you as an individual doer and motivator.

Anyone can be ambitious. Those most likely to realize their dreams are those not only concerned with specific goals and objectives but who have a personal plan in writing! Organizations have a written mission statement and a written business plan. If yours doesn't, you have a great opportunity to help bring them about. And if those two documents exist, insist that they should be made known to every staff member, not just to management personnel. Every member of the team should be familiar with the purpose for existence and the plans to fulfill the ongoing mission.

Goals and objectives must accompany strategies and tactics. Understanding the "why" as well as the what, when, and how will provide employees with a greater incentive to do a job well, not just perfunctorily. Training too often is centered on the proverbial laundry list of tasks.

Do you have a mentor? Are you a mentor? Too many staff members feel "alone" and in a swim or sink atmosphere. No wonder some in the lower echelons feel it is "us" and "them."

If a mission statement and a business plan, plus strategies and tactics, are tools of value to an organization, doesn't it make sense that an individual could benefit by having a personal road map?

Isn't it obvious that the ability to communicate effectively up and down the organization, as well as sideways, is an essential quality for those who would stand out from the crowd? Subtlety may be okay up to a point, but it won't attract the spotlight. You have to do your dance—that's what you get paid for. But if you want progress and a more significant role in the cast, a move upward, you have to do more—you have to perform beyond the norm. The word "do" shows up quite often, doesn't it? Being smart isn't enough. Success comes with the doing!

Perhaps your attention and an in-depth look at the policies and procedures of your organization might seem a bit presumptuous for one in your slot on the organization chart, but isn't the idea to move up a slot—and then two? Some might think you brash. Others, more importantly, might see you as ambitious and talented. One thing is for sure—you can make yourself noticeable.

A "guideline" may suggest a direction. You can and will adopt or adapt and design your own career map. Share your creation with appropriate supervisors and you will be viewed as a trouble-maker, a thinker, a comer, executive material, or maybe a combination of said traits and characteristics. You will be acknowledged as one with substance and, it should be stressed, one with a personal style.

If you already are a CEO, even a quick review of the following could stimulate one or two questions worth addressing.

What is the current usage, the sharing, the awareness, and the application of your written mission statement, written goals and objectives, written business plan, written strategies and tactics, and written company policies?

What else might well be examined? It's a daunting but worthwhile task to look at and evaluate these items:

- Written (and agreed upon!) job descriptions
- Written procedure (and other handbooks?)
- Employee indoctrination and training programs (educational assistance?)
- Facilities, equipment, tools (whatever is appropriate here)
- Performance evaluations (are they "routine" or meaningful and productive?)
- Supervisory talents in interviewing, hiring, evaluating, promoting and firing
- Telephone manners
- The quality of letters and memos
- Ongoing analysis of product, service, cost controls and profits (!)
- Comparison with competitors and peers (with emphasis on market share)
- Research and development
- Marketing (advertising, sales, incentives and promotion programs)
- Public relations (media, community, region, market area,

industry, more?)

- Regulatory and legislative activity, needs, awareness, lobbying
- Efforts surveyed, internal and external, maybe using professional shoppers to evaluate and compare with competitors

Finally, a fair measure of your organization's performance is the reputation enjoyed among your peers, others in your trade or professional society. When you and others in the organization participate in conferences and conventions there is a "feel" as to how you are regarded.

When you ponder the answers and get insights into what you might do to stimulate specific improvements, you just might become even a more valuable asset to the organization. Let's assume your current position is a potential springboard to a higher position. No matter where you are on the totem pole of management, you can present ideas and proposals that will gain attention from those whose perceptions will have a bearing on your advancement. You can implement a style that will illustrate your substance and mark you for greater responsibilities.

You can see to it that those working with you are motivated to contribute to the organization—thus to their own growth and worth. If you are head of a section, a department, or a company, you set the tone and values for those in your sphere of influence— and maybe beyond! Imagine a boss with this plaque on the wall: "You can hire hands and employ others to work *for* you. You must win their hearts to have them work *with* you." Such a plaque was on the wall behind the desk of my first career boss.

In many cases the best route to promotion is to follow your boss up the ladder. If your superior is what you believe a boss should be, then it is in your best interest to help—maybe even push—that boss up the ladder. Such a boss will foster your growth. Who is most likely to be the successor to that boss? You want it to be you. That is, if you are management-oriented as opposed to being a research analyst who prefers to continue working alone in a laboratory. There is a need for professional specialists as well as the executive type. You know which type you are, and you know if you are a potential leader and if you are on the right career ladder. Some who know they are in the wrong slot are reluctant—or too cowardly—to risk change. As the General Electric company's byword of yesteryear said, "Not all change means progress, but there can be no progress without change."

As a sage once asked: "Why not go out on a limb? That's where the fruit is."

Dale Carnegie course instructors say, "Act the way you want to be and soon you'll be the way you act." When I was in my mid-thirties I was approached by the chairman of the board of a hospital. "We need some young blood on our board," he said, "and we'd like you to join us."

Flattered and curious, I asked, "Would you mind telling me why you and your members are inviting me to be the choice?"

"Because," he said with a smile, "among other things, you walk like you have someplace to go and something to do."

A mental flashback gave me a smile. Early in my career I once was chided, not too politely, for having missed a section of a revolving door in a large Chicago office building. For several years I observed that no one going into one of the several revolving doors ever missed an opening. I relaxed a bit in my lifestyle when I moved to a midsized city later, but a habit had been formed.

Perhaps your personal development program will be enhanced by broadening your reading habits. Mystery stories or romances might be relaxing and thus worthwhile, but not be truly profitable if at the expense of keeping up with the trade and professional journals in your field. There is a sure-fire way to stand out from the crowd. Authorship of an article in a trade or professional journal—or even in a local newspaper—will add to credibility and acceptance as an authority. Inclusion of such an item in your resume package (more about this later) can be a real plus!

Self-promotion may be a term thought by some to be crass, but isn't that what career life is all about? Your personal and professional reputation will benefit by such a simple thing as media coverage of your talk before a service club, a trade organization, a conference, a convention—well, you get the idea. You can "arrange" for such coverage by providing a bio and your topic or title, with a few words of explanation, to the master or mistress of ceremonies in advance (!) of your scheduled appearance on the platform.

Wire service coverage and media interviews for broader consumption might come later, but just as "All politics is local," most national successes start with performance and recognition locally. Those in corporate life may have—and should use—help from the in-house professional public relations staff. Bringing yourself to the attention of those people could result in fringe benefits never previously imagined.

Where can one's talk be heard and thus contribute to one's career advantage? How about anywhere and everywhere? At home? The way one talks to a spouse, offspring, and friends and neighbors is observed, even if in a subconscious manner.

Conversation is a social lubricant. Most people are polite and prefer to not be controversial. There are those who admonish their children to avoid religion and politics. Too bad. Those are two of the most conversation-stimulating subjects to many of us—when participants know all involved will be mannerly and not easily offended. Discretion is essential, of course. There should be foreknowledge that those in such a conversation know how to disagree without being disagreeable.

People are judged by what they say and how they say it, whether at a dinner party, a parent-teacher assembly, or a precinct (or ward) meeting. Judgment of listeners is inevitable when one is speaking from the platform or from behind a microphone or in front of a camera.

Speaking up can be a negative. One Sunday afternoon a lady berated her husband for a perceived misplay in a regional bridge tournament. She was not content to simply point out his error, but she made it clear it was not his first. She embarrassed him mercilessly. It was a most unusual scene for the usually sedate, occasionally staid, and sometimes stuffy intellectual players who haunt the bridge circuit. Monday morning she was interviewed for an executive position in a city thirty miles from the scene of the bridge tournament. Small world? She hadn't crossed paths with the interviewer, who had been seated a few tables away from her louder than normal "conversation" with her husband. The interviewer found reason not to hire the one who spoke vociferously when silence or a discreet aside would have been more appropriate.

Attitudes are reflected in the words and style in which they are delivered. Some people develop—and deserve—a reputation as whiners, complainers, and negative critics. Others are known to be upbeat and inclined to recognize and praise positive deeds, skills, and behavior. It is obvious which individuals will have kind words said about them—and who knows when a kind word might have an impact on one's career?

At the staff or committee meetings everyone is expected to have something to contribute. That means the confidence to speak up is significant.

How about the industry conference committee meeting or at a convention? Young comers, mid-management personnel, and seasoned leaders participate in these. Those who are now or who expect to become leaders speak sooner or later, seldom or often, and make an impression. The skill and confidence one exhibits in a group setting can impact career growth.

Those settings are pretty routine. Being a competent platform performer is a step up—a way of standing out from the crowd. Most masters of ceremonies, panel moderators, conference leaders, and officers of organizations begin their platform and microphone mastery as conversation participants, and then as guest speakers.

Listeners sometimes learn something!

Anyone can benefit by being a keen observer of others—a critic, in the positive sense of the word. The average rate of hearing is four times faster than that of speech. To be a good listener, one must concentrate. Here are some tips:

- Listening is not relaxing. It is work, just as if "the meter is running."
- Summarize mentally what is being said so you will be prepared to ask appropriate questions.
- Do not dismiss ideas with which you disagree. Later discussion might prove to be clarifying.
- Do not assume you can fill in the blanks of what wasn't said. If the picture is not clear or complete, a question or request for elaboration may be in order.
- Refrain from premature evaluation of what's being presented until the speaker wraps it up. The conclusion may make things clear.
- Note the tone as well as the words. How a speaker says something can be a clue to the depth of feeling about the comparative importance of a specific point. The "how" of delivery can provide an insight into any biases or prejudices the speaker may have. The agenda may be subtle.
- In participatory situations, nod in agreement when you can. "I see your point" or "That's interesting" encourages elaboration. You are listening to learn, not to try to upstage the main performer.
- If you hear something that is incorrect, downright false, or only partially true, be tactful in making a correction. The speaker may have been misinformed by others, with no malice or intent to mislead. However, to permit an untruth to go unquestioned or unchallenged is cowardly. It is to lie by silence. Many people hesitate to challenge an authority figure, but a tactful question can at least assuage the conscious of the timid.
- Restrain yourself. You'll get a turn. An interrupter may be tolerated but is seldom appreciated.

It might be fun—possibly even profitable—to practice better

listening habits in one's own family settings. Yes? (Here's where you, hesitantly, nod in agreement.)

When you're listening, make comparisons. What worked? What didn't? Visit with speakers socially before a meeting and professionally after, meaning you can then extend a compliment as appropriate and ask a question or two—and then listen! That can be very flattering to a speaker—interest in how he or she got to be an expert or at least exceptionally knowledgeable in the area discussed, and then maybe in what techniques seem to work best. Be as direct or indirect as you deem appropriate. You'll have a feel for establishing rapport and discretion, being interested but not intrusive, attentive but not depriving others of participation. A reputation as a good listener will help you be heard when you speak.

Aristotle said, "It is not sufficient to know what one ought to say, but one must also know how to say it." We might add "...and when to say it."

No matter your skill level on the platform, your conclusion will be one of your most memorable utterances. Just as you knew what your opening sentence would be, so are you prepared to deliver the point toward which you have been driving. Your terminal point is more than just a stopping point. No matter what your purpose, you want to leave cleanly and crisply. You want to leave them laughing if your role of the moment is to entertain. You want to leave them satisfied, whatever else your purpose. It may be you want to leave them motivated to take the desired action. If so, ask for the sale. Get all the commitment you can muster.

Never conclude with "Thank you." If you've done well, your audience's applause will thank *you*!

An aside: I cringe when a professional interviewer on television thanks a contributor for his or her "time." If that's all that was contributed—what a waste!

Writing can be another rung on the ladder.

Getting published is no snap, but it is possible. If one has something worthwhile to say, there is an audience for it. Yes, one has to be egotistical enough and resilient enough to shrug off rejection slips from editors who return form memos or letters saying, "This material does not meet our needs at this time." One would do well to do the necessary market research to see what type of publication prints articles on the subject(s) in your area of interest. *Writer's Market* and Google come to mind.

If you have expertise or can develop expertise in any given field there are editors hungry for your words of wisdom, information, or entertainment. Even getting rejection slips will contribute to your career growth. I think it was Bacon who said, "Reading maketh a full man. Writing maketh an exact man." It might be added that "Speaking maketh a successful man." (Okay, remember, Bacon wrote when the word "man" was generic and meant mankind, meaning females, too. There is no word in the English language that is neuter gender.)

Writing requires the organization of thought, obviously. That discipline contributes to success on the platform. Many beginning speakers feel it necessary to have pages of written copy on the lectern or tabletop before them. If so, copy that is double-spaced and all caps permits a glance to get or keep one on track. Initially, that may be acceptable in one's early efforts. However, never should one read a speech! After a modest amount of experience those same speakers will graduate to use of an outline and then to three-by-five cards with key words only. With more experience and the confidence that comes with it—plus some memory techniques we will discuss later—those same fearful beginners will become hams, using no notes at all. An exception: when quoting more than one statistic, no matter how well they are known, a speaker would do well to refer to the written word just to lend credibility.

Although reading, writing, and speaking are significant elements of success, one should keep in mind that they, along with knowledge, are adjuncts to action, the doing! Opportunity exists in our daily lives. Before one can expect to become a competent public speaker, one must become a competent conversationalist. I once referred to a friend as an interesting conversationalist. I was corrected, by another friend, appropriately. "He is interesting, but he is not a good conversationalist. He's a good talker, but he seldom takes a turn at listening."

A speech, though largely one-sided, is still just an enlarged conversation. The approach is influenced by the situation. Talking to a subordinate in the workplace may be more or it may be less comfortable than talking to the boss. Personal relationships and job situations provide real-life experiences. Those experiences—and the subject matter—have a bearing on our comfort level when we are called upon to speak "in public" or to an in-house group. Thus, before talking about speech preparations and delivery styles, we will touch upon a few circumstances—real-life job and social situations—that will contribute to our confidence to address any group.

> *"The real art of conversation is not only to say the right thing in the right place but to leave unsaid the wrong thing at the tempting moment."*

> DOROTHY NEVILL

FOUR

How Adept Are You at Interviewing? Performance Evaluations?

"The key to successful leadership is influence, not authority."

KENNETH H. BLANCHARD

INTERVIEWERS OF PROSPECTIVE EMPLOYEES are the face of the organization to those persons they interview. Not all interviewers have had mentoring or training. Every applicant, employed or not, carries into the community a perception and an opinion of the professionalism exhibited during the interview.

You may have an equal interest in the approach of the interviewee. You may wish to make a career change yourself some time in the future. If you are a supervisor or manager who conducts performance appraisals, you may find ideas here that will broaden your perspective. If you are on the other side of the desk for an annual or even quarterly performance review, you may benefit by taking a closer look at how you respond to praise, suggestions, or even criticism. There will be a few thoughts about improving your job-seeking techniques. The odds can be improved for success by those who hone their oral skills.

A good interviewer has empathy, recognizing that the interviewee feels his or her future is on the line. There should be tolerance for anxiety. Remember the survey saying that the job interview is one of the most dreaded experiences?

Some interviewers are talkers. They may assume that an applicant or employee who is a good listener is respectful and therefore a good learner. That may or may not be true. The good listener may be over-awed—or tolerant!

Some interviewers seem to feel the need to impress the bright young applicant across the desk. That is an unfortunate but all too common trait, according to pros in the field. Good interviewers are questioners and listeners. They might ask an applicant, "Why do you want to work with this organization?" Some ask about hobbies or spare time activities. Care must be exercised here. An applicant may have some far-out hobby in the opinion of the interviewer. So what? Does the fact one is a stamp collector and the other a bowler and a reader have anything to do with the job at hand? A better question is, "What do you know about our company and industry or profession?" Responses provide insights—or even reveal misconceptions—and a better understanding of how the person will fit into the organization. A good fit is on the mind of the conscientious interviewer more than the question about one's IQ or grade point average—unless either is obviously on the low side or the extremely high side, of course. Questions put to the interviewer are clues that a good interviewer weighs. If an applicant is more interested in fringe benefits than in opportunities, well….

Some jobs have a set salary for a beginner, but for executive positions there is usually some latitude in a given range. Negotiations may be the most delicate part of the conversation. An applicant willing to sell his or her talents and services for the low end of the range is not necessarily the best bargain.

Several professional recruiters have told me they ponder a silent question: "Is this a person I would like to introduce to my son or daughter?" However, liking someone—good chemistry—is not enough. It does not justify a mistake leading to the time and expense of breaking in another new staff member. But, admitted or denied, personal chemistry is a factor in the hiring process, especially if there are a number of qualified candidates. Tests may be administered, but in the end it is often impressions and facts elicited in conversation that determine who gets hired.

The questions an applicant asks should register with the interviewer. An inquisitive mind, plus evidence of proper homework, preparation, and job analysis will let one stand out from the crowd. Is there interest in what the job entails beyond the obvious? Is the applicant interested in opportunity for advancement and personal growth? Are there questions asked about training and mentoring? Does the applicant ask about an educational assistance policy?

If the applicant asks questions the interviewer should have covered, notes to such effect might well be incorporated in print or at least mentally for future use. It is suspected that a few executives spend more time trying on, getting a second opinion, and finally selecting the right suit than they do selecting the right employee. Getting the right employee the first time is a money and time saver for the organization. Here are a couple of thought-stimulators:

Know the qualifications needed for the specific position. Review the written job description in advance of an interview. Is it up to date? Responsibilities are often expanded. Duties sometimes change. Some tasks become obsolete.

Make sure the applicant understands and agrees to what the job entails.

It has been suggested that the best way to learn a subject is to teach it. Also helpful is to prepare a speech on a given subject. If you make a "How to Find a Job" speaking appearance before high school or college seniors, you undoubtedly will ultimately invite questions. You are already aware that it is possible for one to graduate from college and still be an economic illiterate. Developers of the curriculum in our educational system might do well to include instructional material on such simple things as how to balance a checkbook or keep appropriate financial records electronically. Many executives believe there should be a required course entitled "The Free Enterprise System and How It Works." It might include sections or chapters on how the stock market operates, including coaching on how to read the financial page and balance sheets in annual reports. Academia could benefit by utilizing more outside speakers from the real world. Self-confident teachers and professors are not fearful of differing perspectives. This setting is ideal for a would-be speaker to volunteer and hone skills while making a contribution to young people still in their learning and training stages of life.

Another subject for the volunteer speaker from the business or professional world to address for the benefit of the high school or college senior is the art of finding the right career slot. It is a given that we do best that which we enjoy most. Not all careers are based on making the most money possible. We all know the difference between the big fish in the little pond, the little fish in the big pond, and the big fish in the big pond—well, you get it. There are different desires when it comes to choosing a lifestyle. Getting leads on career positions—or just plain jobs that promise to lead upward—is pretty easy for those who play around on the Internet and/or go to job fairs. It's the next step that pays dividends. First, it is desirable if not imperative that one should know what one really wants out of life. A career job is a big, maybe the biggest, factor in the choice. If a job, the position under consideration can be approached as a stepping stone to one's lifetime ambition, and then performance and thus success levels are likely to be high.

Let's say you are a sports nut—but not likely to become a professional athlete. What are the career possibilities? How about selling sports equipment as a starting point? Someone has to be involved in the manufacturing process—and in marketing. Maybe refereeing or umpiring is your forte. Coaching? A job that feels like a hobby can be quite satisfying. The young lady who studied agronomy in college is a groundskeeper at the local country club. We have more flowers and shrubs around the course than ever before. She responded to my compliment with "You really can't imagine how much fun it is to get paid for doing what I love to do." That attitude has taken her to greener pastures, a big city country club with a healthy increase in the budget she has to work with—and a significant salary increase.

Maybe you can be an entrepreneur. Working for someone else is good for getting experience, and such a job will provide a living. It won't make you wealthy, but every organization has top management positions. Your ability to communicate can contribute to upward mobility. Somebody has to be the top gun.

In exploring career possibilities, one should seek discussion with those who have "been there, done that." One should check out the enthusiasm level of those currently employed in an organization of interest.

If your talents, background, and skills justify your interest in a specific area or field, great! Even so, advance homework can save years of misdirected effort leading to a dead end. Some students engaged in a job search are amazed and delighted that many old pros respond to queries for ideas. Who doesn't enjoy and appreciate being asked for advice?

It's a good idea to know the rules before intentionally breaking them, or being too creative. It is likely someone may counsel others to limit a resume to a single page. Some of us who've been around the block think that is nonsense. How can you be sure your resume won't be glanced at and tossed into the stack? If it is simply a recitation of your work or career experience to date, your educational achievements, and your physical characteristics, it will not stand out. Being six feet five inches is probably important if you're going to be a basketball player or a tight end, but otherwise it may be something to be enjoyed, but a "So what?" in most positions sought. Most prospective employers will be more interested in an applicant who indicates that previous employment includes having had a morning paper route when twelve and thirteen, showing ambition and responsibility from an early age. There is something in your background that seemed mundane at the time, but there is potential value in having accomplished something unusual.

Even if you are sufficiently enlightened to start your resume with "Position sought" and a summary of how the organization will benefit by retaining your services, the competition for attention is still pretty stiff. Your resume is not likely to get you a job, but it can be designed to get an interview and a shot at your desired position.

Job searching has changed with the advent of the Internet, of course, but some basics remain. Old-fashioned networking with friends and professional contacts can result in better leads than a mass mailing or knocking on a lot of doors. References and recommendations are most helpful and likely most productive, but you still will want to do expanded homework to zero in on those few prospective potential employers where you have no contacts but are most to your liking. Read what you can about your targets—annual reports, sales literature, and employee publications, including handbooks, if any, given to new employees. You can manage to get some. Such research and familiarity will be of value when the interview occurs. A visit to the home office or to a branch can pay dividends. It will give one a feel for the place—and the opportunity to observe actions and get responses to questions asked of one or more employees. "This looks like a good place to work. Is it as good as it looks?"

A furtive glance over a shoulder is a clue. A broad smile and a nod and an enthusiastic response are what you hope for. That isn't a scientific survey, but it might stimulate additional checking. Sometimes there are ways to solicit input from a competitor or from a vendor. More information could prove valuable.

One might do research at the "morgue" of the appropriate newspaper, probably electronically. Queries at the chamber of commerce and/or the Better Business Bureau should provide insights.

If stockholders own the company, a visit with a stockbroker could be worthwhile. "I'm thinking down the road a bit when I hope to do some investing through you. I have three or four companies in mind that outwardly look good. There's the ABC Company (the one you really want to know about), the XYZ outfit, and the Sleeper. If I were to invest in the near future, how would you rate these three?"

You might get no satisfaction from the answer—but who knows? The time spent could prove worthwhile.

Those who engage in sending a resume via snail mail might do well to address it to the president rather than the vice president of human relations or personnel director, or whatever designation exists for the person who normally handles and disposes of applications. Why? Because the CEO might have ideas not yet shared with others. Or perhaps what you submit might even stimulate an idea. You might get lucky and have a talent that fits the idea still germinating. Yes, it's more likely your resume will be forwarded by the CEO to the proper office. If no comment is attached, the recipient may wonder if this person has some special connection. Thus, your resume may get a closer look than others in the stack. No harm, no foul.

Those who have done their homework—researched the organization's reason for being—will have some idea of what's important to the top brass. Your cover letter and your resume will illustrate that you can make a contribution toward the objective. Those who hire others are more interested in their own objectives than they are in yours. Speak and write in terms of their interest!

Those who see resumes of applicants for supervisory or managerial positions above a (usually) specified salary level see varying levels of sophistication. Decision-making is easier if a candidate's resume is so distinctive it jumps out of the pile. Few do. It is assumed, of course, that a distinctive resume reflects a distinct character. Those resumes lead to interviews.

The process of finding a first or a new job merits more consideration and effort than almost any other endeavor, especially if there are family members who will be impacted by the results of such effort. One will want to research growth prospects not only of the organization in question, but of the entire industry.

Timing can be significant. Seniors in college who expect to graduate in June should not wait until spring to begin exploratory efforts. Smart ones start making inquiries and contacts the preceding fall—or earlier. Established employees contemplating a change of location probably have to consider the school year calendar and the impact on youngsters obliged to change schools. Moving in the summer may be desirable—if one has control over or can negotiate the schedule of a move. If one negotiates a move at a future date, it may be desirable to get agreement that the planned move is to be a confidential matter. Some courtesy notices of departure should be thirty days for executives or even mid-level managers and probably two weeks for non-supervisory personnel. One wants to leave with positive attitudes and good wishes from and on the part of everyone in the organization one is leaving. One should resist any temptation to tell off the superior not respected. Does anyone need to be reminded to avoid burning bridges already crossed? Words—even strong opinions—can be solicited from former employers and/or from employees or peers. They can be harmful or helpful. As a wag once observed, "One cannot have too many friends or too few enemies."

September, October, and November are good months for established career personnel to look for employment opportunities. Explorations could lead to interviews prior to the end of a year. It is a time when budgets are being prepared and goals and objectives are reviewed and updated. It is a time when top guns think about how the organization will expand or improve in the succeeding year. Some may have ideas not yet publicized or even shared beyond intimates. That is why it is recommended one should send a letter of inquiry and a resume to the CEO instead of through normal channels. Before such is routed downward it probably will be perused to some degree and coming down from such high office probably ensures it will get closer scrutiny than the routine application. (An aside: Believe it or not, as a personnel director, later titled Director of Human Relations, I have had in my files more than a hundred applications or resumes for a handful of positions. Very few jump out and say "Look at me!")

I repeat: Ignore the counselor who suggests a one-page resume—or any limit on length, format, or content. Do your thing! Sure, the first page may be fairly standard or it may have an introductory paragraph preceding the usual information. If you are a college graduate, who cares where you graduated from high school—unless, of course, you have discovered the person who might employ you is a graduate of the same school "by coincidence." If you are creative, imaginative, gutsy, you'll let your talent shine. Do not feel obliged to stick to a prescribed format. A subsequent page might enumerate extracurricular achievements, such as civic recognition, offices held, awards, leadership activities, chairmanships, teaching roles—whatever could make your spouse proud. Even that is not enough if you have more!

To make your resume stand out, give special attention to the packaging of the supplementary material—samples of your work. How about a zippered binder with acetate or other transparent page holders? The first page should hold your one-page resume—in your own artistic/creative style. The second page, if you are already experienced, is a listing of your awards and organizations in which you held a title, i.e., president, board member, chairperson, director. Maybe it was a student body office, maybe a service club, maybe a conference or convention leadership role. It may look like a sales kit, with pages of news clippings in which you are featured or at least prominent. Add published works, if any, such as in a trade publication, and samples of your work, such as an employee handbook, a technical or policy or training manual, a public relations guide for supervisors, and programs in which you played a role. If other names of known and somewhat prominent people are also on such a list, so much greater the impact. Do not be modest. This quote is repeatable: "If you can do it, it ain't braggin.'"

Interviewers, including CEOs, are just people, same as you and I. People are more impressed by what they can see and touch and ask about rather than by what they hear in the relatively short conversations that usually pass as interviews, which are too often conducted under time restraints. Seldom will there be time for a complete enumeration of your accomplishments. Besides, to present such accomplishments orally would sound boastful. That's why the visual presentation can be extensive. One item of interest stimulates an additional look at what is presented.

Psychologists say that sight makes twenty times more impact than sound. When we remember something the mental image is usually more significant than any words or voices. And yet it is by the spoken word that most communication occurs. That's why the good conversationalist (that includes one's share of listening) who is enthused and animated stands out in a crowd.

Not all job applicants produce something tangible in the workplace. For some there is not a plethora of visuals to incorporate into a personal sales kit. Thus, it helps to make contact with a prospective employer if referred by a credible friend—one who can say honestly that the organization would be fortunate to acquire this gem. That's what networking is all about.

Leads are where you find them—or create them—by searching! The manager of the chamber of commerce in the city of your choice may be guarded, but could be willing or possibly eager (even over coffee or lunch if you are in upper management) to share public knowledge of possible prospects for your talents. A business editor of the local newspaper might be flattered into sharing a thought when you explain that you've been told he or she really has a handle on what's going on in the community and/or region. Don't be bashful!

The wise job-seeker attempting to make a change will have a firm offer in hand before severing ties with the existing employer.

It is easier, especially at the executive level, to land a new position if springing from a solid base. Those who are caught in a downsizing operation are often unemployed several months. That's why one should always have a savings account (or a stock portfolio to be drawn down only as a last resort) capable of sustaining one's self or family for six months.

So—your resume or referral leads to a personal interview. The resume seldom gets anyone hired. What it is designed to do is to pique interest. It is the oral give and take that determines whether it is likely to be a good fit for the two parties. The qualified and alert candidate will nod affirmatively when appropriate, meaning there is honest agreement. The applicant will not interrupt with questions or comments, but will be ready to answer a question or to offer a thought when a pause is a signaled invitation to speak. The key to standing out from the crowd is to be aware of the objectives of the interviewer. In any situation, one key to success is to be sensitive to the other person's interest and to speak in terms of the other person's needs and interest.

Show interest in more details about what the job entails. Is there opportunity for advancement and personal growth? Mentoring? An inquiry about training and educational assistance impresses interviewers favorably.

An inquisitive mind, homework, including inquiries internally and externally, will give the astute applicant an edge over competitors, especially over those who are just looking for a job and a salary. An applicant who knows the role, purpose, and standing among competitors will score points with the interviewer. But— don't overdo it! Do not presume or pretend you know all there is to know.

An alert interviewee will avoid feeling the need to fill a vacuum of silence. It is a technique—or trick—of broadcast journalists to leave a microphone in the proper position of expectation after a politician has already given an answer. The temptation to elaborate is an opportunity. It is the elaboration that too often provides the quote that will be aired, often to the regret of the one who would have been better served to offer nothing more than a simple smile. The questioner's cocked head and inquiring look sometimes elicits that more interesting quote.

If you can say—and you feel it advantageous—that you have another or more interview(s) before you can decide about an offer, fine. Only you can evaluate your bargaining position, which you might wish to discuss with a mentor, a counselor, or a trusted confidante. Only if one is truly desperate should a job offer be accepted if it is not really a desirable position. Those reading this work are unlikely to be in such a spot. If you don't know your worth and value, how will others view you?

Along the way there may be opportunity to convey the message—assuming this to be a fact—that "We're on the same wave length. I'm glad my [chief strengths and aspirations] appear to be in sync with what you appear to want."

There is no set formula for finding a job, for making a career change, or resigning. Be as competent as you know how, as good as you really are, and let it show, hoping the other person(s) involved have the talent to recognize talent.

Evaluating another's performance is an art, not a science, but there are techniques and practices that elevate the art above the routine and too often perfunctory role played. Many otherwise competent and able management people are not comfortable conducting required performance reviews. Too many are untrained and thus unskilled in this area. A supervisor may be satisfied to fill out a form almost hurriedly if the one being evaluated has not caused any problems, gets to work on time, and appears to be working a full schedule with acceptable results. That lets the executive or front line supervisor get back to work deemed more appropriate than this necessary function created by a calendar date indicating it's time for the quarterly, semi-annual, or annual performance evaluation form.

Performance evaluations should not be conducted on Mondays

or Fridays. One may think back to personal experiences. An anxious employee may experience a weekend filled with apprehension—even dread—if looking forward to a Monday session. For some it can border on the traumatic.

If an evaluation is performed on Friday and there are negatives in the conversation, even if remedial actions are agreed upon, it will be unnecessarily an unpleasant weekend for the one evaluated. That's because remedial steps cannot be taken immediately. Potential solutions may be fussed over and rehashed, the unpleasant aspects of the conversation mulled over more than once, whereas an agreed-upon approach can be taken immediately if such evaluation occurs on a Tuesday, Wednesday, or Thursday. In this case immediate action is more satisfying to parties involved than prolonged meditation and possible resentment.

The important next step is a timely review of progress. If praise can be given, great. If not, both parties must accept the probability that someone is in the wrong career niche.

A good evaluator prepares. Pre-planning enables one to recognize that which merits praise and to determine how to criticize an act without directly criticizing the usually unwitting perpetrator. The mood and style of the evaluator communicates whether this activity (the evaluation or work review) is considered important and thus potentially fruitful for both parties. The employee being evaluated may enter the session wondering if his or her job is on the line. If the evaluator expresses the desire and intent for the team (unit, section, department, or company) to be the best, that sets a tone, and enthusiasm is contagious! Team members catch on quickly that it is easier to succeed if others want you to succeed. Interest in—and promotion of—dreams and aspirations of others usually turns out to be reciprocal. The evaluator who is interested in the success of others will be rewarded by their interest in his or her success.

An opening gambit might well be a joint review of the relevant written job description. An employee might wonder, "Why don't

I ever get recognition for this?" Similarly, an employer might have wondered, "Why do I have to remind anyone to do this?"

Job responsibilities change! Expanded activities lead to an assignment that might be carried out in a timely fashion, but it may or may not become a routine and expected part of the job. If likely that a new function will be repetitive, an updating of the job description is appropriate so the next person occupying said position will know what is expected.

Employees being evaluated sense whether the boss is interested in them as human beings and as individuals. The atmosphere in one-on-one sessions will influence the enthusiasm of the employee and affect future performance.

There are talented people doing whatever is assigned to them, thus never realizing their full potential. A boss might do someone a favor by recognizing a person is in the wrong slot. It's no fun to fire someone, but permitting (okay, encouraging) someone to resign could be a plus for all concerned.

A personal experience can serve as an example. After having for years a less than enthusiastic attitude about government regulators, bureaucrats, and public employees in general, I accepted a gubernatorial appointment and became a bureaucrat. One member of the staff I inherited reputedly would find something wrong with the operation of every financial institution he visited as a state examiner. One savings and loan president complained, "He wears an invisible deputy sheriff's badge on his forehead." That was one of the kinder observations. Other staff members were embarrassed by his attitude, which seemed to be, "No matter how long I have to stay on the scene (with hours of his labor being charged to the institution being examined), I'll find something negative to write up."

I moved up his performance review date. I asked, "If you could be in any career position, what spot would you choose?"

"I'd be an investigator for the IRS," he responded without hesitation.

"You have a degree in accounting. Wouldn't you benefit considerably by being a CPA?"

"Probably."

"John," I said, "it should be obvious to both of us that you're in the wrong career niche. I can build a file to record the necessary three strikes and you're out, and everyone loses. I'll give you sixty days to enroll in courses leading to you becoming a certified public accountant. During that time you look for another job while I can still write a letter that says you have competent technical skills. If you aren't relocated in sixty days I'll have to let you go—with no recommendation."

John soon found other employment with a state agency in which policing procedures were part of the job. Six months later he sent me a sincere thank-you letter. It was a win/win solution. He did ultimately become a CPA!

A winning team needs strong individuals who are team players—and are in the right positions. An outstanding guard on a professional football team is not likely to be an equally good running back. Enlightened leaders and managers conduct exit interviews with departing team members, whether for disgruntlement, a better position, or retirement. Most departing employees, properly encouraged, are willing to lay it all on the table when they know they won't be around anymore. Such straight talk can be quite beneficial. You don't want someone inclined to be bad-mouthing you or the organization. On the other side of the table is one who, if wise, wants to depart with the best possible relationship. After all, prospective employers in the future will be checking past references. In giving a response to a query about a former employee, most respondents are careful with answers. The best question a prospective employer can ask is "Would you rehire?"

An enthusiastic affirmative answer is, of course, the most desired. A flat "no" is unwise and unlikely. A hesitation is an answer, as is "Well, that depends. I really can't give an offhand answer." Without subjecting oneself to a potential lawsuit, one has communicated effectively.

Mad scientists and technical geniuses may work alone, but there's a common denominator in most workplaces: people. The person who can help others realize their potential, inside or outside the organization, is—or will become—a leader.

"We judge ourselves by what we feel capable of doing; others judge us by what we have done."

HENRY WADSWORTH LONGFELLOW

FIVE

Aren't Problems Really Just Challenges?

"Make your program so long and so hard that those who praise you will seem to be talking about something very trivial in comparison with what you are really trying to do."

HENRY FORD

YOU KNOW YOUR JOB. You know your profession and your industry. If you can speak to peers, subordinates, and superiors with credibility in an entertaining manner, you are destined to be a leader outside as well as inside your organization.

When you determine what you want, you could benefit by asking yourself—and perhaps have a confidante assist with another perspective—these questions:

▸▸ What is the current status or situation in this area of interest?

▸▸ What, as exactly as possible, do I (we) want it to be?

▸▸ What are the known or likely obstacles?

- ▶▶ Who is knowledgeable in this area? Can such knowledge be tapped?

- ▶▶ Who will be allies? Who are certain or likely to oppose this direction?

- ▶▶ What, and how valid, are their attitudes, perspectives, and degree of concern?

- ▶▶ What can be learned from known opponents?

- ▶▶ Do I (we) have answers to opposing points of view?

- ▶▶ What and where is additional source material on the subject?

- ▶▶ What makes me (us) qualified to be the disciple(s) of my (our) message?

Answering these questions—and additional research—will assure you of learning something new, maybe more current facts, no matter how extensive your knowledge. You'll develop substantiations of what otherwise might come out simply as bald assertions.

Fervor is an essential ingredient, but even your enthusiasm will not be an answer to objections laced with logic.

Successful persuaders know much more about their subject than they can relate in a half-hour speech or even in a day-long seminar. Probably the most important thing to remember in making a presentation is to keep your audience in mind. If you are giving the same basic talk to a number of audiences, facts won't change, but the way they are presented will. Speeches that are localized and tailored to your specific audience involve audience members more. If your choice of words and use of idioms fit your audience, listeners feel more comfortable with you and understand you more easily, and thus are more interested.

Another important thing to strive for in giving a speech is to win over your audience by encouraging them to like you. Studies have shown that audiences tend to reject the same ideas from people they dislike that they will accept from speakers they like. You need to put across the same good qualities that your friends see in you. If you can project warmth and sincerity without being patronizing or acting like a barker in a cheap circus, your acceptance level will be high.

"Old" facts can still be timeless in illustrating a point. We all quote from the Bible, Shakespeare, Lincoln, Socrates, Mark Twain, and Plato. If you are speaking in St. Louis, you can be sure your audience has heard praise for the Cardinals, the breweries, and the arches. Even old-timers, however, might not know or would enjoy learning that the hot dog and the ice cream cone originated there. How could a city be more all-American? It was at the St. Louis World's Fair of 1904 that a vendor ran out of the white gloves provided customers to eat the wieners or franks too hot to hold in bare fingers. He lamented his plight to a baker friend, who dashed to his shop and returned with elongated rolls. The hot dog was born, although that name came later.

The ice cream cone was also born of crisis—at the same world's fair! Customers exhausted the supply of ice cream dishes and a neighboring vendor came to the rescue. A Syrian gentleman named Hamwi had come from Damascus to sell zalabia at the fair. He rolled some still soft zalabia into a cornucopia. The ice cream cone! Success was instantaneous. When Hamwi died in 1943, he was head of the enormously successful Western Cone Company.

These anecdotes were found in Origins and Firsts, by Jacob M. Braudi. The book is one of the set in the Complete Toastmaster's Library. (Prentice-Hall, Inc.)

The same source provides other examples, from Father's Day originating in Spokane to more numerous firsts in Baltimore, Boston, and Philadelphia.

Ray Cox, then vice president of the Combined Communications Corporation, speaking in Phoenix, got the attention of his audience with this opener:

"I have a friend who is the largest grower of citrus in the state of Maine. Now that may sound a little strange. One doesn't usually think of Maine as being a citrus-growing state. Well, it isn't. And my friend is the only citrus grower in Maine. His grove, if you call it that, is very small. Two grapefruit trees, two orange trees, and two lemon trees. But the fruit he gets from those six trees supplies his family, year-around, with beautiful citrus. Right there in Eagle Lake, Maine, on the banks of the Allagash River.

"And how does he do it? How does he grow such beautiful citrus? Obviously he grows them in a greenhouse. He creates a climate that is conducive to growing citrus. And that's what I want to talk to you about today—creating a climate.

"And I want to talk to you about some things going on in America. Not what's wrong with America, but what's right with it!"

He created a climate of acceptability for his message. Localization will be a plus to your level of acceptability.

On-the-job experience develops and hones expertise. You've seen the scenario more than once. Someone says, "We oughta do something." That usually stimulates a thought, an idea, and a suggestion. The maker of the suggestion is likely to be appointed or nominated and elected to chair a committee to make that something a reality, a happening. A growing experience occurs, a personality blossoms, and it is likely the birth of a speech will follow. If you enjoy attending conferences and conventions around the region or even the country, be the one to motivate the group to a course of action to achieve something of interest to the specific group.

Education may be a factor in establishing credentials, but even those who can add Ph. D behind their names must deliver to motivate! Most of us have to augment our work experience with extensive reading to become expert on any subject. Knowledge is power only if it puts into action, into the doing, the accomplishing of an objective. Some reading material confirms what we already know. Other reading stimulates our imagination for what might be, what could be, and just might inspire a reader to say "It will be!"

Of course there is more to "talking up your ladder" than the ability to make a speech. Leaders do not stay in the box or even inside the lines. They either step outside the boundaries that define their career positions or they are pushed out or pulled out. Leadership qualities will be revealed—assuming they exist—in those who speak up and motivate others. Silence may be golden when it is appropriate to hold one's tongue, but silence rarely moves anyone toward a desired end.

People assume that an orderly presentation of facts reflects an orderly mind. They are inclined to be receptive to the notion that such a presenter can bring order and satisfactory culmination to the opportunities, problems, or challenges at hand. Remember when you opened your mouth to make a positive suggestion and you were given more responsibilities? Congratulations!

When one performs competently behind the microphone, on the platform, on camera, or at the head of the table, leadership opportunities, even demands, are forthcoming. Invitations to speak at functions will be followed by invitations and urging to serve on and then chair committee meetings, to conduct business meetings, conferences, even conventions. Some will be invited to serve on boards of directors—even on boards that pay a stipend for each meeting attended! New career paths open and even beckon those who train themselves to be competent in serving at center stage, thus in a position to motivate!

Al Jolson, one of the stars of vaudeville in the 1920s, received sound and lasting advice from his father when the five-year-old was making his first tap-dancing appearance on stage. The theater projectionist handling the spotlight from the booth in the balcony had trouble at first in finding the small body moving so rapidly. Al tried to dance toward the light. When the boy finally exited into the backstage wings the father smiled and slid a hand on Al's shoulder. "Son, when you're on stage it's like life. You just do your act and the spotlight will find you."

Spotlights come with varying degrees of light and heat. If you can communicate orally and inspire others, the spotlight is likely to find you. If you authenticate your expertise by getting words published, such as in your trade or professional journal, you will be assured of being in demand. The minister of your church may ask you to head the fund-raising drive for a new wing or to head the every-member canvass—because you have proven to be a motivator. Your service club members or the chamber of commerce nominating committee may start an arm-twisting campaign. Political activists may try to persuade you to run for elective office. Be careful what you want. You might get it!

Readers will undoubtedly observe that my chapters are of differing lengths. I am reminded of Lincoln's answer to "What should be the length of a speech?" His answer: "A speech should be like a lady's dress. Long enough to cover the subject but short enough to be interesting."

So—to would-be leaders who logically expect a conclusion pertinent to the subject of motivation, I leave you with an appropriate concluding poem by Edgar Guest, thought of by many as the common man's uncommon poet.

It Couldn't Be Done
by Edgar Albert Guest

Somebody said that it couldn't be done
But he with a chuckle replied
That "maybe it couldn't," but he would be one
Who wouldn't say so till he tried.
So he buckled right in with a trace of a grin
On his face. If he worried he hid it.
He started to sing as he tackled the thing
That couldn't be done, and he did it!

Somebody scoffed: "Oh, you'll never do that;
At least no one ever has done it;"
But he took off his coat and he took off his hat
And the first thing we knew he'd begun it.

With a lift of his chin and a bit of a grin,
    If any doubt rose, he forbid it.
He started to sing as he tackled the thing
    That couldn't be done, and he did it.

There are thousands to tell you it cannot be done,
    There are thousands to prophesy failure,
There are thousands to point out to you, one by one,
    The dangers that wait to assail you.
But just buckle in with a bit of a grin,
    Just take off your coat and go to it;
Just start in to sing as you tackle the thing
    That "cannot be done," and you'll do it.

SIX

Ready to Build a Speech?

"Your ability to talk one-on-one can start an organization. Your ability to talk to a small group can ignite a cause. Your ability to talk to a large audience can mount a crusade. You, as an effective speaker, can make things happen!"

R. H. BOB LEWIS

THE SEVERAL STEPS to successful speaking start with credentials. One must have some known expertise to justify having an audience invest time to hear what a speaker has to say. Knowledge of a subject may come from education, training, possibly some research, and, of course, experience and satisfactory performance. Mastery of a subject usually comes from a combination of these factors.

A speaker was asked "How long did it take you to prepare that speech? It was great!"

The answer: "I've been preparing for it all my life."

Aren't you and I living a life that has produced and is producing areas of interest and concern? We all have favorite subjects—even causes—upon which we enjoy expounding.

O. Henry, when asked how to write a good short story, answered

"Think of a good ending and write up to it." That's one way—certainly not the only way—a speaker might start the mental process of preparing a talk on an agreed-upon subject to a specific audience at a specified time and place and for a limited (!) time period.

Elements to be included into a talk do not often come to a speaker's mind in any logical sequence. The thought process can be as haphazard as "That's a point I'll want to work into my remarks—and I sure want to remind the audience of...."

Random thoughts will then be arranged into a logical sequence for orderly presentation—remember the assumption of an orderly mind? Such orderliness, even though the concluding thought may have been the first to come to mind, is reflected in the preparation of the lead (a hook designed to capture interest), the body or guts of the matter, and a conclusion with a purpose!

The only sentences to be committed to memory are (1) the lead sentence after acknowledgment of the introduction and (2) the concluding sentence. Usage of 1, 2, 3 or A, B, C signifies key points and usually helps an audience of either readers or listeners pay special attention.

Prior to the introduction on the platform the chairperson, sometimes also the one who serves as emcee, hopes and tries to stimulate and/or assure maximum interest in your appearance and message. *Who* is delivering the message is often the best selling point for attendance and attention. Qualifications and credentials will be used in advance publicity and promotion, primarily from material you will have been asked to provide. That will also be the basis of the oral introduction. Be factual and not unduly modest. Do not be surprised if editorial elaboration is appended or intertwined in material you provide.

What the subject is has a strong bearing on audience attendance, interest, and initial attention to its merit. The emcee will know the speech title, which should give a clue as to what the topic is, and also should be acquainted with the importance of the subject matter if he or she is to do a credible job of making the introduction. More on the role of an emcee will be discussed later.

Nervousness is not uncommon in beginning speakers. It is not necessarily a bad thing to experience the feeling of butterflies in the stomach. The trick, simply stated, is to get them into formation. One sage suggested visualizing one's audience as a gathering of the naked. That might be dangerous—especially if individualized. It is far better to think of audience members as friends—most of whom may be strangers waiting to be your friend. As someone said, "To have friends, be one."

After you acknowledge the gracious introduction, and possibly express pleasure at being before the specific group, the hook—your lead sentence—is set in the first thirty seconds or maybe one minute. That's the time the ordinary listener takes to determine if the speaker and subject merit maximum or casual attention. The hook may be a challenge, a startling statistic, a germane question, a teaser, a quotation, or the most delicate tool: humor. A professional comedian will utilize humor, of course. That's his or her stock in trade. For the rest of us, well, we'd better be good. A joke is dangerous. What if it falls flat? Nothing is guaranteed. The speaker who is confident, proven, and has experience assuring the success of a humorous incident, may use it if it illustrates a germane point and does not need to stimulate a belly laugh.

Immediate impact is desirable, be it a gasp of shock, a laugh, or most often an affirmative nodding of heads, literally or figuratively. A provocative question, an utterance displaying near anger, an anecdote, a warning, a rumor (be sure to identify it as such), a threat, a purpose or a goal, an obvious exaggeration, a demonstration with a prop (more later), even a fairy tale or something astounding and/ or ridiculous can be used as an attention-getter. Your personality and your style will determine a comfort zone with the approaches you choose with various audiences.

"No profanity" is an excellent rule. Potentially offensive language is usually employed only by those lacking an adequate vocabulary. Imagine—a preacher startled his congregation in the airless church by booming, "It's a goddamn hot day!" Did that startle more than a few? Did it grab everyone's attention, even the youngsters who had been thinking they'd rather be out playing? Confident he had attention, the minister immediately launched into his sermon. "That's what I heard a blasphemer say yesterday!" His Bible-thumping message illustrated he knew how and when to break a rule. The wise know the rules they break.

Localizing your opening gets your audience on your side at the outset. (Yes, there's some repetition here.) For example, if you were to speak in Denver, a timely subject might be introduced thusly: "According to the publication, 'The Top Ten of Everything,' you people in Denver have less obesity than any major city in the United States. Congratulations! That indicates you are active people, and that helps with what we are going to talk about today."

A speaker in Seattle opened with this: "I have been struck by a contradiction about your beautiful city. It was once declared the 'most livable.' It has experienced a couple of high profile riots, an earthquake, the departure of Boeing headquarters (to Chicago, several years ago), but you have taken all that in stride and have bounced. That's impressive. Oh, yes, you have some challenges in traffic. The contradiction, however, relates to weather. Despite common perceptions, Seattle doesn't even come close to being in the top ten cities in the U.S. in annual precipitation!" (Then came a pregnant pause.)

"In your state you do have the rain forest on the Olympic Peninsula, which does rank tops, but just across the Cascade Mountains, less than three hours from here, we find that Yakima ranks as the eighth *driest* city in our nation. Without Grand Coulee Dam and irrigation, Central Washington would be a desert. These facts illustrate the dangers of generalizations. I want us to be *specific* about some things today...."

A speaker can assure attention by presenting a mental picture. "You are the coach and general manager of a professional football team. You are keenly aware of the two longstanding weaknesses in your defense. You've been on a tight budget, but the team owner has told you to take whatever steps necessary to make this a winning team."

That lead stimulates the audience's mental participation. It was a natural lead for a speech entitled "You're the Boss. Do You Need to Fire Someone?" Publicity announcing a title can create conversation, maybe even apprehension, but most assuredly, expectations this will be a hot topic! The speaker offered counsel on the termination process, as discussed earlier in this work. That speech was part of a seminar with the theme, "Building a Winning Management Team." The speaker continued with "In professional sports, players either cut the mustard or accept the fact they are on the way out. Should it be any different in running your business?"

As mentioned earlier, a talk may be opened with a prop or visual aid appropriate for the audience. Maybe this one for a country club banquet after a golf tournament: "Look at this pitching wedge. A simple tool. Right? Well, maybe it's simple for Tiger Woods, but for us with, oh, say handicaps of ten or higher, it's anything but simple. With this tool and the net we have set up, our pro has agreed to hit balls from this mat and give us a group lesson, free! You low handicappers be patient and restrain yourselves to smiles and 'Amens,' please."

The following opener is good for any assemblage of management personnel. "Can anyone in this audience stick this ordinary straw into this ordinary potato? If so, please come forward and demonstrate." The speaker is accomplishing three things: (1) Attention is guaranteed. (2) If someone comes forward and sticks the straw into the potato, that person has center stage and receives acclamation as the one person in the room who knows how to meet this particular challenge. This is a lot better than the speaker doing it and having someone in the audience say with a smirk, "Big deal. I've done that a lot of times." (3) If a volunteer is successful or the speaker does his trick, the point is illustrated: "Give the job to someone with the necessary know-how or show your staff members how to do it."

It is rare anyone in the audience knows the trick. The volunteer or speaker jabs the straw into the potato. "Here's how I did it—I pinched the straw two thirds of the way toward the top end. Air in the straw is compressed, not being able to escape at the top of the straw, and thus it is as if I were jamming a piece of steel into the potato. What's my point? As managers you either have people who know how to do the job you want done or you are obliged to see to it they have the know-how and the tools to perform at the one hundred percent level, at their full potential."

Props or visual aids can be comforting to the novice speaker as well as being functional for the pro. The first moments of a talk might be considered the appetizer of a meal, as if it were a shrimp cocktail. The body of the talk is the entrée, the main course, maybe steak and lobster. The conclusion is sweet, the dessert of one's choice.

Getting the audience hooked with your opener isn't guaranteed to be enough to keep everyone awake, especially immediately after lunch. As we agreed, comedians are entertainers. You most likely are on the platform to inform, educate, persuade, and maybe sell. You will want to present facts and reasons for action or acceptance *in an entertaining manner.* Those who do so are likely to enjoy return engagements and referrals to other organizations in need of speakers.

A word of warning: Incorrect grammar can distract listeners from the content of your message. Most of your audiences are likely to consist of people who are fairly well educated. While correct usage of our language is important, overemphasis or illustrating your knowledge of big words could make you appear stilted. Winston Churchill is said to have once used a word he was asked to explain. With good humor he did, and added, "I use a big word on rare occasions just to illustrate that I do know one or two."

To be sure, there is more to platform performance than good grammar, structure, and content. There's flavor, style, life, sometimes humor, and above all, organized enthusiasm! If all goes well, there is enjoyment for both the audience and the speaker.

To repeat: Novice speakers, initially, may feel it necessary to have a printed script on the lectern. If one is needed, it should be double-spaced and in all-caps. The speaker will want to glance at it only occasionally—and certainly not read it! The comer will soon progress to three-by-five cards with a vertical listing of key words, each designed to stimulate a paragraph or two of verbal presentation.

The more advanced speaker will learn memory techniques (to be discussed later) but will never (!) try to memorize a talk. One should master the content, of course, and practice or rehearse, possibly in front of the bathroom mirror or, better, before an honest spouse or trustworthy compatriot. The practice of delivery ensures improvement. Two caveats: (1) Do have complete mastery of the first sentence to be uttered after acknowledgment of the introduction and (2) Do have firmly in mind your concluding sentence. Dynamic—or even just competent—speakers have a destination point, a clean decisive ending. (So you read this earlier. Advertising commercials run more than twice. Maybe you can remember a couple?)

Body language impacts the acceptance of your talk. A stationary microphone, seldom used today, limits one's range of motion, so hands and face are visual communicators of the animated speaker. A portable wireless mic is the favorite of evangelists and comedians. Gone are the days when one would distract the audience with the crackling of the whip like a lion tamer while strolling across the stage with a trailing cord. The neck mic or miniature mic clipped to the lapel or collar for the television interview is soon forgotten by all. Most of us know that fiddling with the mic can cause static. Enough on that aspect of our platform performance.

There are times, as stated earlier, when even the professional speaker *should* refer to notes or even to a publication, if that is the source of more than simple statistics being quoted. Why? To lend credibility and thus avoid challenges or questions, asked or unasked, by potential skeptics. Another time to refer to written material is when quoting a public figure with more than just a few words. This is especially true if members of the media are present or if anyone in the audience could be hostile, such as at a political function.

You have probably gone to the library or Internet to check out sources of quotations. When offering anecdotes, witticisms, or whatever, be sure to credit the original author or speaker. There are those in the audience who are well read, and you do not wish to be charged and found guilty of plagiarism.

If the main point of your speech has been communicated, received, and absorbed, the sale of whatever you are pitching is there for the taking. But—you have to ask for it! Audiences are most likely to remember the first and/or the last thing they heard. Even a good speech is ruined if it drifts into nothingness, such as, "Well, I guess that's all. Thank you for being a gracious audience."

I repeat: Never thank an audience! Your listeners should owe thanks to you for a message of interest and importance in an entertaining or challenging manner. Even the politically hackneyed "God bless you all" is better than "Thank you."

As Jay Leno says, "No mercy applause, please." With your final words you have a choice: Leave them laughing, leave them fighting mad, leave them hungry for more, leave them sold on your ideas, product, or service, but whatever you do—leave them not dangling, but cleanly!

The emcee and the speaker will determine before the talk if there is to be a question and answer session after said talk, but when you finish your talk, be finished! Sit down to accept deserved applause. Do not remain standing and say "I'll now accept questions." If you do, some in the audience will have started clapping and then pause and figuratively stutter with embarrassment. Let the emcee announce that you have agreed or consented to entertain questions. During a Q&A period a point not clear that is in need of embellishment can be clarified or elaborated upon. Mention of a question and answer period in the emcee's introductory remarks sometimes sharpens audience interest, especially among those who might wish to reveal their knowledge of the subject or just be capable of asking a pertinent question.

In small groups the logistics are easy. However, if hundreds are seated at tables, such as at a luncheon or dinner, it may be efficient to have three-by-five cards distributed in advance for written questions to be collected and delivered to the speaker. That eliminates the need for microphones. The competent speaker will repeat a question for the benefit of those out of earshot range of the questioner, asking from the front of the room for example. You don't want someone shouting "What was the question?" We've all witnessed that. Sure, the speaker catches on after only one such outburst, but it's a negative event. This happens even in select circles. For example, even at press briefings conducted by the president's spokesperson. No one wants an answer to go out to a television audience without the question being clearly understood by all.

My speaking of the question and answer period has stimulated a mental picture for me of an event of the distant past—several decades ago. A speaker who was in a leadership position in the U. S. Senate was addressing a couple hundred or more Chicago Executive Club members at a luncheon held at the LaSalle Hotel. That senator pulled a trick that merited my admiration for cleverness and my disdain for its deception. Part of an overflow crowd was seated at a table between the swinging doors to the kitchen and the rear of the podium. That gave at least two of us at that table an almost rear-view look at the speaker. Members of the audience were invited to write their questions on the cards provided at their tables. These were gathered by two of the senator's aides and delivered to him. He pulled a relatively short stack of cards from the shelf under the slanted part of the lectern, presumably not in sight of any audience members, and tucked the newly received cards under the one blue card at the bottom of his previously stashed Q&A cards. He then read questions and gave concise and intelligent answers. He elaborated at length his answer to the question on the card that was the last before the blue card. That answer was on "...a most pertinent and important question," he explained, as he went into considerable detail—right up to the time for adjournment. Even though I relate the story, it is not with intent to belittle an outstanding public servant, who later served as ambassador to Japan. (Not Speaker Tom Foley. See? Old-timers and history buffs are given the opportunity to feel a bit smug, knowing the name of the senator from Montana.)

You want to leave your audience in a changed state of mind. You leave them informed, entertained, and inspired. You leave them laughing, crying, challenged, ready to take action, maybe even fighting mad, but most important, you leave them sold on your concept or your idea—motivated and ready to do something about it!

Fred Vest, who was later in New York in a top position with Dale Carnegie and Associates, was once my mentor and golfing buddy in Spokane, Washington. He was retained by a firm to deliver a motivational talk stressing the importance of not just positive thinking but also of enthusiasm in performing one's job. For his conclusion he picked up a half-filled glass of water from in front of the seat he had occupied next to the lectern. He gave credit to Mark Twain for the quote, "Anyone can be enthusiastic for thirty minutes. Most of us can be enthusiastic for thirty days. Those who will succeed are those who can be enthusiastic for thirty years."

He raised a half-filled glass of water, one of three that had been on the shelf of the lectern, out of sight until withdrawn, and dropped an aspirin into it. "Notice," he said, "how the aspirin flakes off briefly and just lies there, almost dormant? It didn't show much." He paused, then said, "Now let me point out, with emphasis, that I make no comparisons to the medical value of the products I'm using for this illustration." He then poured Bromo Seltzer into a second half-filled glass of water. It bubbled furiously for a few seconds and settled rather unattractively. "Like Bromo Seltzer," he grinned, "most of us can be enthusiastic for a short time, then we are inclined to relax and settle back." He sat the glass down and brought out another. He again held the glass at eye level and dropped an Alka-Seltzer tablet into it. "Notice how it twinkles and effervesces—and twinkles and effervesces!" He sat the glass down and paused. "Now I ask you—how are you living your life and performing your job—as an aspirin, a Bromo Seltzer, or an Alka-Seltzer?"

This illustration should satisfy all that there are appropriate closings for any theme or subject. You can create or you can borrow. This timeless one is by an attorney, which should show that despite the jokes not all attorneys are bad guys.

My Creed by Dean Alfange

I do not choose to be a common man. It is my right to be uncommon—if I can. I seek opportunity—not security. I do not wish to be a kept citizen, humbled and dulled by having the state look after me. I want to take the calculated risk; to dream and to build, to fail and to succeed. I refuse to barter incentive for a dole. I prefer the challenges of life to the guaranteed existence; the thrill of fulfillment to the stale calm of utopia. I will not trade freedom for beneficence nor my dignity for a handout. I will never cower before any master nor bend to any threat. It is my heritage to stand erect, proud and unafraid; to think and act for myself, enjoy the benefit of my creations, and to face the world boldly and say, this I have done. All this is what it means to be an American.

Our closings reflect something about us. That makes them quite significant!

You must ask for the sale—make it easy for people to take action. If you want them to join an organization, have membership applications distributed on cue. Maybe you have several pre-sold and coached to make enthusiastic comments, as mundane as "Gimme that! I'll sign it." If you want volunteers do not hesitate to use shills. Some people don't like to take the first step but will join a parade.

Especially if you plan to have audience action or participation, you must have a planned terminal point—final words with impact that close your portion of the program cleanly and decisively! A "take this action!" admonition. Never a weak "Thank you." Use a sentence that makes the audience thank you—with applause!

Providing information is not likely to be enough to make you a dynamic speaker. You don't want to walk away from an audience wondering "So what?" Information does not ensure action. Any speaker who speaks only for applause from others needs to be reminded of these words by Oliver Goldsmith:

> *"He who seeks only applause...has all his happiness in another's keeping."*

SEVEN

Would Memory Techniques Help?

> *"Reading is to the mind what exercise is to the body.
> By the one health is preserved, strengthened,
> and invigorated; by the other, virtue, which is
> the health of the mind, is kept alive, cherished,
> and confirmed."*

SIR RICHARD STEELE

MOST PEOPLE never learn how to study. If one owns a book, phrases can be underlined and notes can be made in the margins, or one can highlight the most significant sentences or paragraphs. An introduction to the use of acronyms was a big deal in my studies in college and later in my public speaking. If that technique had been familiar to me in elementary and high school, my grades, which were pretty good, would have been better.

Acronyms? SCUBA divers probably are among the few who can rattle off "self-contained underwater breathing apparatus." We use language shortcuts daily, often without realizing they are acronyms. For example, RADAR: radio detecting and ranging; and the SWAT team got its name because it uses special weapons and tactics. We all know OPEC stands for the Organization of Petroleum Exporting Countries and MADD is a shortcut for Mothers Against Drunk Driving. We've watched MASH—or reruns about a particular mobile army surgical hospital in Korea. Doesn't everyone know that NATO originally stood for North Atlantic Treaty Organization? Its expansion might require a new acronym.

The simplest example of assisted memory-recall by use of an acronym is this: Name the Great Lakes. Look away from this page a moment and name them.

Okay, welcome back. Many readers will recall the teacher who taught them to use the word "HOMES." Those readers smiled and said, "Huron, Ontario, Michigan, Erie, and Superior." Easy as that.

Key words can be the basis of an acronym that can be of invaluable assistance to a public speaker or even to one studying for an examination. Let's say you are to speak to a service club. Your goal is to get members of your audience to be donors to the development of a neighborhood playground and a petting zoo. Yes, it's an easy subject to use as an illustration, but you will get the idea and then adopt and adapt the technique to your subject matter. Obviously, someone has interest in the project or you would not have been invited to speak to these influential citizens. You will have lobbied or will lobby the directors, and you and they want member support with, of course, maximum dollar participation.

Kids, animals, and the American flag rank highest among many advertisers in their efforts to arouse acceptance, action, and/or empathetic or maybe even sympathetic feelings. Most members of your service club audience are parents or grandparents. Your lead, the hook, may incorporate nostalgia. "Remember when you were a kid? If you lived in a big city you may have had to play in the streets. If you were a country bumpkin there may have been no park or playground other than the school yard. If you lived in a small town there may have been one city park, possibly even with a swimming pool. If you were lucky enough to live in a town or city with a cohesive park system you have fond memories of playtime."

In preparing the body of your hypothetical pitch for a park and petting zoo, the elements include land acquisition and equipment for the playground. You visualize fenced areas and buildings for domestic animals with walkways that permit the kids of your city to reach over or through fences to pet sheep, goats, calves, and maybe ponies. Maybe you'll get the local humane society interested enough to put puppies and/or kittens on display—for affection and possible adoption. You will be speaking with enthusiasm that does not come with the reading of a script! You want to, as always, exhibit spontaneity, even apparently restrained excitement. Obvious sincerity comes easier if one is speaking without notes. Your role is to create more than enthusiasm—you want to stimulate action! You still will want orderliness, which listeners assume reflects an orderly mind. By creating acronyms you can present ideas in your desired sequence.

Look at the elements of your message and select or create key words that you will ultimately arrange into an easy-to-remember acronym. Logically, land acquisition is a primary and initial concern/objective. Thus, we start with the word "Land." That single word enables you to speak the necessary number of paragraphs on that facet of your proposal. The first letter is "L," so we have the starting point for our acronym. Now we need a vowel. Equipment gives us the letter "E." You won't have to refer to notes to remember what the "L" and the "E" stand for. Surely the words "Animals" and "Petting" will trigger the mind to think of ponies, calves, lambs, goat kids, and whatever else (puppies? kitties?) you will propose to be in your menagerie. So—the letters LEAP form your acronym. From that one word you are prepared to pitch your audience for twenty minutes and have five or ten minutes for questions, suggestions, and whatever audience participation you want to stimulate, presumably more than mere acceptance. You want an endorsement of your proposal. You want pledges of action and dollars.

Okay, that was so simple it may be discerned as having been too easy. Any speech you make will have a theme, a main point to be driven home. Such a talk can be divided into cohesive units.

The opening, along with your lead sentence and paragraph, will establish your theme. The orderly units lead you and your audience members to a logical conclusion. There may be half a dozen units, or eight. Whatever. I recommend ten as a maximum. You start by making notes of the speech you plan to deliver. You familiarize yourself with the key points by reading and rearranging and elaboration or elimination. The modifications you make will lead you to a well-prepared and logical sequence with appropriate emphasis where desired. You will not be reading this speech. You will be speaking extemporaneously—not a term to be confused with the word "impromptu," which means spur of the moment, presumably unplanned, without formal preparation. Of course, if you are called upon to address a subject, it is because you are recognized as one who has, over a period of time and exposure, mastered your subject at least to the extent others want to hear what you have to say about a matter of mutual interest.

Let's imagine you are invited to speak about your recognized success in utilizing your employees as front line public relations ambassadors for your organization. You know that audience involvement assures interest, attention, and appreciation. That often simply means mental involvement, which keeps the audience not only awake but also alert and receptive. You want agreement and possibly action. A useful technique in the following example would be to present a mental quiz, as opposed to your recitation of your personal successes in the area under consideration and possibly later discussion.

After thanks to the emcee for the gracious introduction, your appropriate and rehearsed lead segues into the body of your talk. You explain that a starting point is to evaluate, with a point system, where the organization being considered—or each individual's organization—is today. Responses here are to be mental, thus at least temporarily private. You emphasize that "No matter how outstanding your employees are in specific areas, ten points is the maximum anyone can claim for each answer. We do not want some of you to lose credibility by ending up with more than one hundred percent."

You may choose to elaborate on each question, making a series of mini-speeches, but for purposes of developing an acronym as a memory aid, the raw questions comprise the written worksheet you developed in preparation. Once on the platform, you may wish to reassure your listeners that you have confidence in their ability to keep a running mental score, but "…it will not be considered cheating if some choose to privately jot down the numbers as we go along."

(Note to the reader: In my framing of these questions you may assume, correctly, that I had to change a word or two to achieve what was needed to form an acronym. The italicized words were underlined after those changes. It was necessary to rearrange the sequence of a couple of the questions. Things do not fall "automatically" into place for me any more often than they will for you.)

1. **Policies** and the development of a business plan are based on your written mission statement and your business plan, which includes written goals and objectives, sometimes even tactics. Are these elements known and understood at every level—and agreed upon?

2. **Individuals** should agree that written job descriptions are current.

3. **Training** is an ongoing program. Is current attention in your training field adequate?

4. **Determination** to perform at peak levels leads to success. Are you motivating and inspiring such determined performance?

5. **Open** door policies sound good. Are open conversation opportunities more realistic than those too-often phony words?

6. **Customer** relations is everyone's responsibility. Does your training include handling the disgruntled customer?

7. **Telephone** manners matter. Does your telephone company offer training seminars?

8. **Oral** orders often lead to written correspondence, which

reflects your image, whether by letter or e-mail. How does your organization rate on the oral part?

9. **Relationships** count. Are you and key employees relating to and active in community affairs? (Chamber of commerce, service clubs, lobbying?)

10. **Storytelling** is meant here as getting your message out to the public. Paid advertising is essential, of course, but legitimate news is also welcomed by the media. This area may be assigned to a pro, but individual employee achievements, civic contributions, and human interest activities are stories that can be related to that pro with suggestions for usage. Do you have a story to tell?

The first letter of each numbered unit creates the acronym PIT DOCTORS. That may sound ridiculous, but the more ludicrous something is, the easier it is to remember. You will surprise yourself by remembering that "P" stands for "policies" and that one word will lead you into your lead paragraph. The "I" for individuals, and onward. Yes, you will have to review and familiarize your memory with the elements of Pit Doctor—and pleasure will come from the mastery you will enjoy! You noticed, because of the bold type, that in your preparatory material a key word serves as reinforcement for your memory peg word.

There will be a smile if you add, "Okay, here's a bonus question worth ten points: Do you really care about all this? Enough to take positive action?"

In developing the acronym as your memory aid, innovation counts! As we search for key words, we recognize a need for a mix of consonants and vowels. This is not as difficult as it might at first seem. Play around with the system and you will get dividends. (I know—during your first presentation you might need a cheat sheet.) If the first letter of each key word forms an acronym, so much the better. You will deliver points without having to look at your visual aid. That impresses listeners and viewers, maybe for some only subconsciously, but some will be aware of your talent.

Your interest in this material shows you have ambitions. Thus, it is quite likely to make a difference in your direction and personal career development.

If you hope to advance your career by improved platform performance, or maybe even earn income for speaking appearances or by conducting seminars or writing articles, you will want to be more than knowledgeable. You'll want to be colorful, with both substance and style. The payoff is in enhanced prestige—and even enhanced income!

> *"It's easy to make a buck. It's tougher to make a difference."*
>
> TOM BROKAW

EIGHT

How Comfortable Are You When Conducting Meetings?

"Good enough" is never good enough for real leaders!

R. H. Bob Lewis

Meetings for a specific purpose are more likely to result in success than are those meetings called because it is "time to have a meeting." Obvious? Would a few phone calls or a couple of one-on-one visits accomplish the objective?

Too many meetings are attended by people who have no business being there. They may resent the waste of their time. They may feel obliged to participate—and thus waste the time of those truly involved in the subject on the table. So—before calling a meeting, one should determine the following:

1. What is the nature of the business to be discussed?
2. What is the objective?
3. To whom should invitations be extended? This may lead to dangerous temptation, when one considers who is likely to be supportive, who is likely to be in opposition, and who will be undecided but objective.

4. Who will be offended if not included—and what is the cost/benefit ratio?

5. Would the distribution of a tentative agenda, stating location, time, duration, and subject matter provide opportunity for needed preparation by participants?

Efficiency is measurable in the eyes of every participant. The competent presiding officer will consider these points:

a. Have an agenda—made available to all!

b. Start on schedule.

c. Know something about parliamentary procedure. (The need varies.)

d. Be capable of handling the unexpected.

e. Be friendly and enthusiastic—and fair!

f. Have a terminal point and arrive there on schedule.

If members of a group know that meetings traditionally start on time, they'll appear on time. If the starting time is known as a joke, they'll drift in at their leisure, preferring to be there when the action starts rather than having to wait for latecomers. Thus, they may contribute to that which they deplore, often vocally.

Formal organizations operate and conduct business sessions under rules of order if members desire orderliness, direction, fairness, and achievement. Boards of directors, service clubs, conventions, societies, and formal committees consider Robert's Rules of Order preferable to winging it.

General Henry M. Robert worked three years on the last revision of his classic manual, published in 1915. It doubled the size and rendered obsolete his edition of 1893. The revised and updated version edited by John Sherman and published by Barnes and Noble in 1993 streamlines language that had become archaic. Those who have handshaking acquaintanceship with Robert's Rules of Order will get along very nicely in most circumstances. Those who serve or desire to serve as presiding officers (referred to in the neuter gender as "chairs") will do well to devote a bit of study to the subject. As practice under guidance usually helps, participation in a Toastmasters club is recommended as being highly beneficial. The offering here will be more than superficial, but is really meant to encourage real-life experience.

The way to open a meeting is to get everyone's attention by use of a gavel, although in less formal settings a utensil tapped on a water glass is deemed acceptable. (You can guess which I would prefer.) Then, "The meeting will please come to order." If a quorum is not present, a competent chairperson will get the message across by gaveling on schedule, then announcing after the call to order, "The chair declares a recess until a quorum is present, but the secretary will please record the starting time and the length of the necessary recess." Members will get the idea. One club I spoke to levied token fines for tardiness and a humorous report, almost biting, was part of the opening ceremony.

An agenda ensures orderliness. (That doesn't mean stiffness!) It usually means there is a call to order, sometimes a flag salute in the form of recitation of the Pledge of Allegiance, sometimes an invocation, maybe a recitation of a creed or even the singing of the national anthem or an alternative. Speakers go with the flow. The introduction of guests, if any, usually would come next.

- ▶▶ Then, normally, comes the reading of the minutes (or dispensation thereof)
- ▶▶ A treasurer's report (seldom stimulating questions, but they are legitimate)
- ▶▶ Reports of standing committees, with discussion as appropriate and directed
- ▶▶ Reports of any special committee(s), resulting in appropriate action
- ▶▶ Old (or unfinished) business
- ▶▶ New business

- ▸▸ Program
- ▸▸ Announcements (These sometimes are scheduled immediately after reading of the minutes. Circumstances and judgment dictate.)
- ▸▸ Adjournment (On schedule!)

The above is a guide. It is not sacred. The important thing is for the chair to have a direction and a destination and a sequence of steps to accomplish both. If there is a need to accommodate a speaker's personal schedule, such accommodation is not just a courtesy but often an absolute necessity. Such an adjustment could be especially desirable if the chair knows there could be controversial and lengthy debate about any item on the agenda. It is absurd to break off a heated discussion with a matter unresolved. Who would care to speak in an antagonistic atmosphere? Ongoing debate should not intrude into the time allotted to the speaker! In Japan speakers are put on stage immediately prior to a scheduled meal—to be served at a known specified time. What an incentive for all parties to adhere to the schedule!

So much for the mechanics of efficiency. The objective in your mind is the meat of the matter. Success is never assured, but the odds sure are better if every participant understands the goals. If participants are led to suggest them, the execution of plans will be carried out with more enthusiasm than if action is based on orders from above. A jointly developed plan, an agreed upon timetable, and an understood deadline, with encouragement along the way toward achievable goals, are key steps to desired ends. You, the meeting leader, will get your share of credit, especially if you are generous in recognizing the contributions of others.

Usually the smaller the group the better, as long as it is balanced— not stacked. There can be more relaxed give and take, more openness in small groups. If opposition to your desired end is pronounced, what is the merit to a different approach? What does an opponent really want? Can that wish be accommodated? Is compromise in order?

These are questions successful leaders/managers consider. There may be other factors in your situation, but the above questions still need answers.

Weekly, monthly, quarterly, semi-annual or annual meetings occur because it is time for said meeting and they will occur whether there is a heavy or a light agenda or just a routine schedule. There is usually value in just getting the group together even if only to review common interests, progress, and the future.

So—say at one of these meetings you are the program chairperson or the emcee, the master of ceremonies. Maybe you're to be a panelist or a panel moderator. Ultimately you may be the convention or conference chairperson. The roles have similarities, but responsibilities and techniques differ.

The conference or convention chairperson is responsible for the entire event, thus determining and coordinating the elements thereof. The program chairperson plays a role similar to that of a television producer. The anchor person on TV is on camera in the starring role, but the program content, sequence of presentation, setting, and behind-the-scenes arrangements are what make things viewers see go smoothly. Most functions are fairly routine. It is the unforeseen that challenges—and provides learning opportunities. One experience in my role as the featured speaker stimulated an idea that contributed to the atmosphere of a successful start of luncheons, conferences, and conventions that I subsequently chaired. The president of the Nelson, B. C. Chamber of Commerce apologized during the social hour for what he feared would be a lightly attended annual banquet. "It is Bobbie Burns Night, plus there is a hockey game with Spokane tonight." We were surprised and pleased when the crowd swelled to the extent that a round table for eight had to be wheeled in at the last moment. The chair's evident enthusiasm and member reaction contributed greatly to the atmosphere in the room. From that date on I tipped the caterer or appropriate party to set up the room one or two (if a large crowd) tables short for the expected attendance. But—be ready!

Such a last-minute flurry of activity sets the crowd buzzing with comments about such a successful turnout! That puts the audience in an expectant and receptive mood—a delightful atmosphere for all (especially this speaker).

When you are playing the role of the emcee you are a key contributor, but not the star. You are the oil (without being oily) that makes the machinery run smoothly. You may be tempted to indulge in humor, which is okay as long as you do not fancy yourself a comedian. Use humor illustratively so it is of value even if it elicits only chuckles as opposed to belly laughs.

Your first order of business is preparation. You may be doubling as program chairperson. Either way, you will know the routine—the starting time, the equally inviolate adjournment time, the time allocated for the business portion, if any, of the program, and the allocated time (pre-specified!) for the speaker or speakers. Audience members rightfully expect you to honor your schedule so they can honor theirs.

If you are the emcee but not the program chairperson, it will be assumed you already are, or will be, sufficiently familiar with the format that you adhere to it. Any speaker worthy of the invitation knows the sanctity of schedules—something to remember when you are the guest speaker. If questions are to be entertained at the conclusion of the talk the emcee announces that in advance. The time to be allotted should be agreed upon, again in advance, by the emcee and the speaker.

It will be a rare occasion when a speaker exceeds her or his timeframe, but it does happen. As emcee, you will be seated adjacent to the lectern. You and the audience will be tolerant for about two—maybe three or even four—minutes! You will want to stir at the first sign of a stirring in front of you and the speaker. One technique is to write "Two minutes" on a note and slip it onto the lectern as discreetly as possible—even though we know invisibility is impossible. That will get you off the hook with the audience for the speaker's indiscretion.

Unlikely, but not impossible, is the need for more drastic terminating action. It would be rude to stand to indicate closure is desired, but if an oaf is so indifferent to your written notification, well, if guests are leaving (this can happen), then it may be necessary to whisper, "Can you wrap this up with your closing point?"

When the speaker finally surrenders the lectern, you still are obliged to lead the applause with apparent appreciation. Make a brief positive observation about the value of the message just received before adjourning. Do not say, "Without further ado" ever! If you have played your role properly, there was never any ado. (Look up the word and let the impact of my admonition sink in.) Another "never" is to never thank an interviewee, interviewer, or speaker for his or her time. If time is the only thing worthy of your thanks then it means you think nothing else was of value, that the message was a nothing.

The emcee who is not the program chairperson or top gun of the organization still may be part of those involved in the care and feeding of the dignitary, key speaker, or any visiting participant deserving of extraordinary hospitality of the hosts. Sometimes this function is handled by professional staff members, who will take care of everything, but there can be times when you are the host or part of a hosting group. Someone must be concerned about the guest(s) in question. What about travel arrangements? Who is meeting and greeting? Are local transportation needs being met? Will there be an accompanying spouse or staffer? Are hotel accommodations more than adequate? How big a deal is this? Should there be flowers and/or a fruit basket in the room or suite? Should the spouse be hosted to an outside activity (or activities if more than a one-day stay)? Will the guest(s) be in and out or present for the length of the conference or convention? If there is a speaking or seminar fee and/or expenses how will payment be handled?

The program room set-up is worthy of your interest and maybe your direction, depending upon the role you are playing. Microphones are one concern. The size of the crowd may merit strategically placed microphones for a question and answer period. Roving handheld mics are more likely—and more desirable! The person presiding should be aware of the possible need to repeat questions asked from the floor if there is the slightest chance some in the audience are not in a position to hear the soft-spoken lady in the front row.

Name tags are often helpful or even highly desirable at many functions. There is a preferred position for name tags, and it is not the left breast pocket of a suit or blouse. Visualize yourself shaking hands with a new acquaintance. You are tall; your new friend is diminutive. It is awkward to bend and cock one's neck to see the name. The natural sight travel of people shaking hands is to the upper right breast! That's where it is recommended name tags be, and the typeface should be larger than the ten point font of a typewriter! Readers shouldn't be obliged to squint.

The competent emcee will have secured a biography of the speaker(s) and will arrange, if feasible, an advance visit for a more personal relationship and an insight into the character of the person(s) and subject matter perspectives. Indulge me, please, as I relate a personal experience at a speaking engagement years ago. Clark Lewis, then mayor of Longview, Washington, and known as somewhat of a curmudgeon, was the master of ceremonies. I was a city councilman and then vice president of the Association of Washington Cities, promoting an initiative to the state legislature. The audience was comprised primarily of mayors and council members from municipalities of Southwest Washington, but also present were a number of county commissioners and state legislators.

We met, as arranged, in the lobby of the Monticello Hotel half an hour before the dinner meeting. Mayor Lewis said, "Bob, I have read your standard resume from the mayor's office in Spokane, so I know you're a graduate of the University of Missouri and vice president of AWC and chair of the initiative to get cities a share of the sales tax, but I want something more personal. Tell me, are you a Virginia Lewis or a Massachusetts Lewis?"

"Gosh, I don't know. I've never traced my family tree, but I do know my grandfather was born in West Virginia, so I guess his family came from Virginia."

"That's interesting. Meriwether Lewis—the great scout—was a Virginia Lewis. Do you suppose you're a direct descendant of him?"

"I told you—I've never traced my ancestry, but I doubt it. Someone in my clan would be bragging about it."

"Well," the old guy drawled and grinned. "Maybe you're not what some of your political opponents have implied." He paused. "Meriwether Lewis, you obviously didn't know, well, he never married."

What fun that character might have had if I had made a false claim!

The competent emcee does not want simply to recite copy from a puff piece. The speaker is human and should be so presented as one whose credentials justify the attention of the audience. The title of the talk should give a strong clue as to the topic. The competent emcee will stress both the importance and value of the talk to this body of listeners—without making the speech for the speaker!

A tip: Present the title and topic and then the importance before mentioning the speaker's name. Then, at the end of the introductory material, with flair or even near-excitement revealing your personal enthusiasm: "Please join me in welcoming (Ms. or Miss or Mrs.) Susie Jones or Mr. John Smith." Lead the applause, but be ready for a handshake in case the speaker initiates one, as does occur. The TIS formula for introducing a speaker is from a Dale Carnegie class: topic, importance, speaker—in that order. (I don't think I'll be sued for plagiarism when I consider this to be a plug for DC.)

At the conclusion you exhibit enthusiasm by leading the applause, and, if it comes naturally under the circumstances, there might or might not be a handshake. There is no formula—just be ready if the speaker initiates such.

As you develop or have developed your skill as a platform performer you are or will be invited to participate as a panelist or even as the panel moderator. Your preparation will include more than familiarity with the subject. That's basic and assumed. Preparation includes pre-awareness of areas and points that will be emphasized or could be addressed by fellow panelists. It can be distressing to hear a predecessor deliver your speech.

You must be adept enough to elaborate upon or even politely and discreetly add to some of the points made by others. You don't want to come across as a "me, too" person. The able moderator will have the panelists meet in advance to coordinate topics. Otherwise there is the risk of duplication or even omission. It cannot be a home run unless every base is touched. As a pundit observed, "Touching home plate twice does not make up for missing the bag at second."

Graciousness is an appreciated quality in a team effort. Recognition of a different point of view can be handled without one being offensive. The ability to disagree agreeably is the mark of a pro. One should never strip another person of intellectual dignity—unless, of course, you encounter a once-in-a-lifetime arrogant and abrasive attack dog, a pit bull snarling at you. Be the good guy or gal, friendly, self-confidently in control of yourself—and thus the situation! Always stay calm during a storm. You can be controversial, thought-provoking, even dramatic, and keep the audience with you. Smile when tempted to frown. That can be disarming. Be willing to laugh at yourself, agree when possible, and concede a little to gain a lot. Never argue. Debate, yes. Stand firm in your beliefs or risk being thought of as a blowhard or a spineless dullard.

Being adequate doesn't cut it. Your objective is to be outstanding. That's what personal growth is all about. Good enough is not good enough!

As a moderator, you will be more than a referee or an umpire. The moderator, if competent, plays more the role of a coach, motivating and inspiring additional input or clarification, if necessary, from the players.

Initially, in making introductions of the panelists and the subject, the moderator exercises the techniques of the emcee. In advance of the program, rules and procedures will have been shared with participants. They will know time allotments, sequence of appearance, the question and answer format—and no speeches for answers! The rules of the game will be clear to the audience and to the panelists. In some formats panelists may question each other. Some egoists like to make a series of mini-speeches, self-satisfying desserts after the main course. Some speakers may have to be interrupted. The same may be true of questioners from the floor. Courtesy and leniency should be extended to those with expertise who are making a contribution, but there also are know-nothings who employ verbosity.

The skilled moderator will maintain control without hurting feelings. "Thank you—and let us hitch-hike on your thought." Or "A good point, one which deserves consideration by our other panelists" can be a smooth and inoffensive interruption.

In concluding a panel session, the moderator will thank the panelists by name, making eye contact and giving an appreciative nod. The audience should be thanked for attentiveness "...with special thanks to those in the audience who participated and thus contributed to the success of the meeting." The audience may be invited to show appreciation by a last round of applause. You as a platform performer will develop a feel for what is desirable and when and how to make the right things happen. You also will mention, if and when applicable, the availability of tapes, video tapes, or transcripts of the program.

The toughest session for a speaker, emcee, or moderator is the one immediately after lunch. Usually everything will proceed on schedule, but here's a tip if starting on time is obviously not feasible. I was presiding at the 1:30 slot at a national convention in Tahoe. The luncheon program was a really good one, and the emcee let the lively Q&A session run overtime. A number of the three hundred attendees needed to make a restroom stop. Others paused to drop a few more quarters or dollars into the slot machines (pre-paper slip days). About two hundred were present by

1:35. The decibel count was high. I banged the gavel and called the meeting to order. I then said, "Many of you people haven't really met each other. You nod as you pass each other and you check out name tags to see where people are from, but you don't really get acquainted. This meeting is now in recess for five minutes. Please take this opportunity to introduce yourselves to each other. Shake hands and exchange names and a sentence or two with everyone within your reach."

I left the platform and shook hands with those arriving through the nearest entrance, explaining we were in recess pending everyone's arrival. Although some were sheepish, the atmosphere was later described to me as festive. After five minutes I rapped the gavel and everyone settled down. The comments after the meeting were gratifying. Comments included, "It's more fun to sit with friends than with strangers." This proved to be worth doing at later meetings, even when there was no tardiness.

Now to the business of conducting meetings. Surely you will be called upon to play this most important role! Here are a few worthy generalities:

▶▶ Be friendly and courteous.
▶▶ Maintain control, but not be dictatorial.
▶▶ Portray efficiency, competency, and above all, fairness.
▶▶ Have an agenda—a program guide, and a known and stated objective.
▶▶ Start on time and adjourn on schedule.

Starting on time can be a challenge in less than formal settings. If meetings are routinely scheduled from 7:00 to 9:00 p.m., everyone knows that. Yet, at the first meeting at which you preside there may not be the required quorum at the prescribed starting time. It happens. If there is a recording secretary, that person will certainly be present on schedule. Members, present or not, will understand that you intend to be a proficient chairperson if you say at 7:00

p.m., "The meeting will please come to order. Let the record show the meeting was convened on schedule. The chair now declares a recess until a quorum is present."

The moment a quorum is reached, strike the gavel without apparent malice and say, "Recess is concluded and the meeting will now come to order." Your message will have been received. My father occasionally felt obliged to say to my brother and/or me, "I may be smiling, but you know I mean it!"

You will experience various levels of attention or concern about the minutes of the previous meeting. Their importance varies, and in many instances if there was little action or activity of consequence there may be a motion made, seconded, and passed to dispense with the reading of the minutes. You will know what is appropriate for those attending meetings at which you are presiding. In a minority of cases printed minutes of the previous meeting may be distributed in advance of the meeting. In some organizations minutes are in place before the attendees arrive. In the former case it may be assumed members have reviewed the minutes prior to arrival. In the latter case there will be those who may or may not have had time to read them prior to the rap of the meeting-opening gavel. In any event, the motion is in order to adopt the minutes as presented. Still, one should ask, "Are there corrections or additions to the minutes?"

This requires members to have read or now to scan printed minutes quickly (or listen carefully to the minutes if they are presented orally). Some conscientious member will already have spotted or will detect an omission or error if such exists. During the course of the chairperson's term there may be one or two instances in which the minutes prove to be less than perfect. A motion to correct or amend is no big deal. If there are no corrections or additions, the chair should remember that a motion to accept the minutes requires a second, as do most motions. The motion to adjourn is non-debatable. If an unnecessary "Second!" is offered, no harm, no foul. That vote is immediate.

If a correction or amendment to the minutes was adopted the motion should be repeated by the chair with inclusion of the words, "...as amended" or "...as corrected," and voted upon.

Also worthy of noting (for purists) is the fact that nominations do not require a second. Some organizations, especially political ones, invite or at least permit a second (or even more than one) so supportive remarks (or even speeches) can be made. However, most organizations choose to operate under Robert's Rules of Order. It is well for a chairperson to be familiar with the basics. One does not want to be overbearing in the application of such rules, but a good chairperson will want to know enough to avoid being embarrassed by some smart alec opponent. (We'll touch on severe hecklers later.)

Those in legislative bodies operating under Reed's Rules of Order and/or House or Senate special rules will become familiar with them—or risk public embarrassment.

The treasurer's report? Again, if printed and distributed, that's one thing. Formal settings of larger organization may practice this as a routine matter, but some organizations are so casual the treasurer might say, "We're solvent," and that may be adequate. Such a treasurer, however, should be prepared to encounter the new kid on the block or a wiseacre waiting to raise questions. (Anyone you know?)

Standing committee chairpersons should be called upon for reports even if there is nothing to report. Oblige the chairperson to go on record saying so. There might be a legitimate question out there. No one should have to be aggressive to learn the status of a pending function or activity.

Obviously, a special committee will have something timely to report. Ad hoc or special committees usually have a specified lifespan and a single assignment.

The presiding officer must be aware of those wishing to speak, but the committee chairperson may be granted the role of handling questions regarding the matter at hand. Beware of a discussion becoming so informal it becomes a bull session. The competent presiding officer will not let members interrupt each other. There are people who would intimidate others and speak without recognition by the chair. A presiding officer can maintain control by saying something like, "Just a minute, John. Susan has the floor and Dave had his hand up before you. We'll get to your turn in a minute or two." It can happen that John persists in interrupting or making side comments. To that person the chair might have to say, "John, please let Susan finish. We all will get a turn, in an orderly fashion, please." You will endear yourself to those who play by the rules. It may be necessary to rule once in your entire career, "John, you are out of order. Please be seated and seek recognition of the chair before speaking again." If John becomes a problem, I trust you will encourage (request) his friends take appropriate action—probably to take John for a walk. Keeping it as light as possible, you might say, "John will enjoy an excused absence."

Old business and new business, it will be assumed there are distinctions participants know. It may be necessary, on occasion, to remind a forward-thinking member that the item she or he is bringing up will be discussed "when we get to new business on the agenda." Mere reference to the agenda strengthens the role of the presiding officer.

Under old business or new business the chair may be inclined to provide a direction if no one is indicating a desire to speak, and may accomplish such by taking the lead with a statement like this: "The chair will entertain a motion to (state purpose) if you would like to have the body consider this. Discussion will then be in order." There is a reassurance of fairness in the statement that discussion will then be in order. This is also a reminder that the chair expects operations to proceed in an orderly manner. It won't take long for all to be aware that business will be conducted properly, not as a bull session.

If ever a motion is made and a second is not readily forthcoming, ask if there is a second. If there is not, ask again. If none, the chair should announce: "The motion is lost for want of a second." When a motion is made and seconded the secretary will record in the minutes the motion and the name of the maker of the motion and of the one who seconded it. If numerous seconds are offered simultaneously, the competent secretary will simply select one of the more prominent voices and credit that person as being the one. Discussion and disposition of the motion follows.

A motion to delete or add sequential words to an original motion is simple. "I move to delete the words (state them) which appear after the words (state them) and before the words (state them)."

The same procedure applies if one wishes to insert words. The motion is now, "I move to insert the words (state them) after the words (state them) and before the words (state them)."

A second is required before debate is in order. If the chair asks if there is a second and there is no response, the chair asks again. If no second is forthcoming the chair states, "The motion is lost for want of a second." If there is a second, debate is in order. When debate is deemed by the chair to be complete a vote is called for those in favor of adopting the motion to vote "Aye." If the vote is decisive, even unanimous, the chair still asks for those opposed to vote "No." The chair then announces and the secretary records the result.

Parliamentary procedure is more formal in some organizations than in others. You have to determine how adept you must be in the field and pursue education accordingly.

The chair should consider it to be desirable or even necessary to restate the proposed amendment so it is clear to all. Discussion of the proposed amendment is appropriate. Such discussion should be allowed until it becomes obvious adequate discussion has occurred. If exhaustive debate ensues, some impatient soul may say, or even shout, "Question!" That is not an appropriate approach. Recognition from the chair should be sought and obtained, then, "I move the previous question." (A second is required.) If the chair believes discussion is over, it usually is acceptable to say, "I believe we are ready to vote on the proposed amendment if there are no objections (pause—and if none) we'll now vote to accept or reject the proposed amendment."

If even one member indicates a desire for further discussion, the motion moving the previous question is before the body and must be voted upon. An explanation from the chair is usually desirable. "Those in favor of an immediate vote on the motion before the body please so indicate by saying, 'Aye.'" Pause to accept the yes votes. Even if the outcome is obvious, it is appropriate (I'll even say necessary) to ask for the negative or "no" votes. Then announce the outcome. If, after someone moves the previous question a participant expresses a desire to continue debate, then the chair says, "The previous question has been moved and passed (if so), which, as you know, terminates debate on the proposed amendment." If the "no" votes prevail, the chair announces that further discussion is appropriate. Assuming the amendment under discussion ultimately is passed, the chair says, "We will now vote on the motion as amended. The secretary will please read the motion, as amended, now before the house."

If there is any doubt possible about the number for and against a motion, the voice vote should be followed by a show of hands. The chair and the secretary do the counting and the chair announces the agreed-upon numbers. The count should be recorded in the minutes.

An amendment may also be amended—but only one amendment to the amendment! If someone should naively offer an amendment to the amendment to the amendment the chair will rule such an offering as "Sorry, that's out of order. Only one amendment is allowed to an amendment."

Any motion in conflict with the bylaws or constitution of the organization must be ruled out of order. Those who are destined to be presiding officers will find the offering of a substitute motion relatively easy to handle. The most important assets of a chairperson are courtesy, fairness, and the ability to stay cool when under pressure.

Reading these words may suggest a course of action, but it is in the doing that we become at least competent—with the goal of becoming "most competent."

A search via Google will provide current offerings in this field, such as Rules of Order for Association Boards (1997); Democratic Rules of Order (7th edition, by Fred and Peg Francis); and a look at Wikipedia, The Free Encyclopedia, which points out something I didn't know—that most state legislatures follow Mason's Manual of Legislative Procedure. (When I was a state senator in Washington we used Reed's Rules of Order.) The U.S. Senate follows Standing Rules of the United States Senate.

Most organizations still use Robert's Rules of Order. That's what you are most likely to find useful. Those who want to really become professional in this field might wish to research the National Association of Parliamentarians and the American Institute of Parliamentarians. Let me emphasize—those organizations are for the Pro's, with a capital "P."

"I have but one lamp by which my feet are guided; and that is the lamp of experience."

PATRICK HENRY

NINE

How Comfortable Are You in Dealing with the Media?

*Let me have access to the channels of publicity
and I care not who makes my country's laws.*

THEODORE ROOSEVELT

YOU'RE INTO YOUR ACT and drawing attention. Internally, your organization's editor of publications should find your public appearances of interest. A feature story about your platform activities should easily be arranged, if not by you directly, then by your supervisor, your mentor, or just by an interested friend. You do not have to be a schemer to get legitimate coverage, but don't be overly modest. You may or may not have heard or read the saying, "Blest is he who tooteth his own horn lest it not be tooted." You weren't born a leader. You had to—or have to—do something. Ideas may be great, but they are nothing if not implemented.

Your trade or professional journals have been—or should be—made aware of your exploits, accomplishments, and speaking appearances. Either you or the staffer in charge of public relations, publicity, or advertising either has seen or must be encouraged to see to that. The local press will be on top of any news you make if aware of it, preferably in advance. Both the print and broadcast media will cover your activities, your words, and, yes, your warts and goofs. Leaders and doers are newsworthy. Civic and volunteer organizations are utilizing or will utilize your talents. Giving generously of yourself, serving (!), is a major part of being a success in this game called life. As one sage expressed it, "Service to others is the rent I pay for my space on earth."

When you say something, reporters and columnists usually urge you—by their questions—to explain further if clarification or elaboration seems desirable. Seldom will you be interviewed by a reporter fighting a deadline, but it can happen. Knowing how to be terse without being abrupt is helpful. Radio news reporters or local talk show hosts may record your remarks, or you may be live behind the mic and/or on-camera. Reporters often are obliged (by respondents too "wordy") to edit remarks and select those words that reflect your message accurately and honestly. Assume this until you are controversial and in danger of innuendo or editorializing by someone who stoops to slant the news. That danger, I fear, does exist occasionally. Excerpts lifted out of context can make one look better or worse than merited.

The live television interview is the most challenging, the most potentially helpful, and thus the most dangerous. If you can consider the interviewer a personal friend, which is possible, you have a head start. Such relationships can be legitimately cultivated. For me it was easy if such friends enjoyed a hosted golf game. Handicaps even things up in golf; one doesn't have to be very talented to enjoy the game. It's tougher for tennis players, who have to be more equally skilled to enjoy a match. The point is, whatever works for you. Fishing? Boating? Poker? Barbecuing? Use your imagination. One can learn quite a bit about a person during golf or poker games. Being acquainted—or just more aware of likes, temperaments, dislikes, prejudices, ambitions, even family life—can pay dividends.

Prior to a scheduled television interview or live program as a panelist can you anticipate the likely questions? The position of others who might be involved? Can an associate help you prepare, even to the extent of commenting upon proposed answers you plan to offer to controversial issues? Routine questions might have a twist to them to the listener not familiar with the subject matter. You can strongly influence the direction of the interview. Watch and learn from the professionals you see on cable and network television. You will hear such deflections as "That's a good question, but what we should be addressing here is...." That ploy should not be overused, obviously. The best answer is a straight-forward one, of course, but if the direction is not to your liking, don't sit there and take a beating! A wrong answer is a lot worse than "I don't know." Truth is your best weapon, no matter how smart you think you are.

Your notoriety, fame, recognition, acceptance—whatever—will be enhanced if your organization's public relations staff (possibly a single individual) is pushing you out front if you have the ability to make the organization look good. Your looking good is a positive by-product for the PR staff or individual. If you are an independent operator without a PR staff you might inquire of the president or manager of the local chamber of commerce as to whether the media might be interested in what you are pitching. If you are a member of a service club or appear occasionally as a speaker at such there are or will be a couple of members keenly interested in and impressed by the messages you are delivering. Do not be shy about requesting help in getting your message out. They belong to and will suggest to other organizations that you are a good program. One speaking engagement will lead to another. (To illustrate: A Pennsylvania president of a data processing firm was in the audience for a seminar I conducted in Boca Raton. He engaged my services, a half-day seminar and an after-dinner speech, for his firm's succeeding annual conventions in Annapolis, Boston, and at Hilton Head.)

You have targeted audiences. Getting someone to suggest you

as a speaker or as an interviewee can be the difference between going somewhere or just sitting there hoping someone will notice you. Don't wait for Opportunity to knock on your door—you knock on Opportunity's door!

Style is something most people have to develop. We are not born with much more than the ability to learn. Even the naturals strive to polish their talents. That's one of the reasons you are reading these words. Asking the appropriate questions and seeking the help and cooperation of the right people will lead to contacts beneficial for a lifetime. Some of your friends and associates have contacts that will surprise you. Letting them help you, just as you are willing and eager to help them, shows that you respect their judgment and expertise. Years ago I had a friend who was anchor man in the news department of a local television station. He shared his recipe guaranteed to make the interviewee look at least as good as the interviewer. Some tips of yesteryear are valid forever. I saved and now share the recipe of a longtime friend, Bob Briley:

1. Do not agree to an interview if you are not thoroughly acquainted with the subject matter.

2. Before the interview, try to get a line on the basic questions to be asked.

3. Be prepared. You have fifteen seconds or less at the beginning of the interview to establish your image, authority, and credibility. Set the tone. Start with a summary statement, not the interim facts used to reach a decision or position. If you feel it would be helpful, commit your opening sentence to memory. (You can handle one sentence, but do not try to memorize more.)

4. During the interview sit in a comfortable position so you can breathe easily.

5. Try to keep your body relaxed and as immobile as possible, keeping hands still (occasional gestures are okay) and not touching the microphone or cable.

6. Ignore the camera (!) until you become comfortable

looking at it while talking.

7. Concentrate on the questioner, especially on every word of his or her question.

8. If the question is phrased or worded in such a way as to be unclear, don't be reluctant to ask for a clarification.

9. If the question is preceded by a statement to which you take exception, don't be afraid to refute it (if possible) or at least challenge its validity.

10. Make answers as concise as possible without omitting relevant thoughts on the subject.

11. If you don't have an answer to a question, don't be afraid to admit it, but add that you will find the answer. (Then do it. What you do with it will require off-camera agreement.)

12. This is my editorial comment: It probably would be a good idea to reread the above before your next interview.

Do not ask or expect to preview a print story or a broadcast interview. You probably will be aware or made aware of when the telecast of your interview will occur. Do not ask when a print story will appear. If timely, it will appear shortly. A feature story will be used when the appropriate editor feels it is appropriate, maybe tomorrow, maybe Sunday, maybe....

One's "philosophy" or attitude about press relations should be based on certain precepts. If you can accept and adopt these, you'll probably be ahead of most competitors.

A reporter has a job to do. That reporter is a human being, possibly less than perfect in every aspect. They would like to believe they are objective, and they usually try. (Many are not, some openly so, some subtly or even subconsciously.)

News is supposed to be factual. It is difficult—and dangerous—to improve upon the truth. Openness, character, and credibility will determine one's reputation. Remember, "I don't know" can be the most honest and thus best answer. "But I will find out and get back to you." Do. (Yes, I'm aware you've heard that before.)

If one is providing news or is news, all the facts are fair game. If (when) an error occurs, it probably was inadvertent, either an accident or a misunderstanding. Never threaten to call a superior! A polite question is usually preferable and will get a more favorable response than a demand for a retraction or correction.

Years ago a sage pointed out that it is dangerous and foolhardy to hit, physically or verbally, a person who uses a typewriter (now a computer), a camera, or a microphone to earn a living.

Keep in mind that you and the reporter are subject to the vagaries of the hurried, harried, or careless headline writer. Under the pressure of time and space headline writers often read only the first two paragraphs of a story to get the background for a headline and sometimes also a subhead. We all have read stories that started in an obvious direction and then took a turn or twist with the use of "but" or "however." Such a shift can lead to the creation of a distorted headline, and is not the fault of the reporter who interviewed or just wrote about you. He or she simply forgot to put the disclaimer early enough in the story. Don't fret or fuss—unless national security or human life is endangered it will pass as an unfortunate incident.

Publicity can be good or bad. Advertising is purchased. Editorial writing is opinion and perception. Know and respect the difference.

It's okay to be disappointed if only a portion of your remarks are printed or aired, but it's not okay to be discouraged or to complain. Space and time limitations are often beyond the control of the well-intentioned interviewer. You do not want the reputation of being a whiner or a griper. Do not thank someone for doing his or her job—but, appreciation is okay in the form of congratulations for a job well-done. There is a difference, subtle as it is. Oh, yes, do not grant an interview and then say, "Now the part about…is off the record, of course." If you and the reporter or interviewer agree to a background discussion, well and good. That means you trust each other and probably will be helpful to each other.

Remember, news staffers are just people. Specialists, yes, but human. They want to have good rapport with news sources and news subjects so they can enjoy ready access and trustworthy input. You, as a newsmaker, want the best rapport possible with those who present you and/or your words to the public.

Your good works and contributions may or may not be considered newsworthy. Do something outrageous, stupid, or crooked, and you may be sure you will be noticed. Your good works will reflect favorably and you'll bask in the notoriety. But—no matter how good or how careful you are, they can cause you distress or even pain if they are so inclined! In fact, even to come under suspicion for wrongdoing can get you a lot of bad publicity.

For example, a state regulator was sued by a contractor who claimed the regulator was in cahoots with the savings and loan association that foreclosed on the builder in the middle of construction of a seven million dollar building. The way it happened was shabby at best, unethical but legal. The builder was developing his project with quarterly advances from the financial institution. When such cash advances were unexpectedly discontinued, he couldn't make monthly payments on his loans to date. He, of course, should never have put himself in this position, but neither would a responsible lender engage in such an arrangement.

What the builder didn't know was that the regulator, based on findings by his regulatory staff during routine and then special examinations, was trying to put some of the so-called perpetrators out of office and into prison for other actions. An examination is not to be confused with an audit, which is done both by internal staff members and by an independent accounting firm. By law, a regulator cannot disclose any findings made by staff examiners—except when so ordered by a judge. The builder's case was thrown out of court. He appealed to a higher court and lost again. However, he took his story to the media. A television station and its sister radio station gave him air time. He maligned the bureaucracy viciously for not protecting him from the officers and board of the financial institution. He formed a "Committee to Keep Banks Honest." A neighbor, the owner of a television and a radio station, reportedly donated twenty-five thousand dollars to get the ball rolling. The builder testified before state legislative committees and got great news coverage but no legal satisfaction. The committee members agreed with the findings of the courts and the attorney general that the regulators (sometimes popular targets, even if not legitimately so) had performed properly. Appropriately, they did not try to upset or overturn a civil lawsuit. The builder enticed a national network television program producer to take an interest in his complaint. Had he taken a different approach, he could have had the moral support of the state regulatory staff, but he chose to malign and sue everybody, including the governor.

Smelling blood—or wanting to—the producer saw a little guy taking on the big, bad bureaucracy. An interview with the regulator was set up. If the regulator declined to comment for the program, he reasoned, the presentation would be more one-sided than it already was predestined to be. "No comment" is seldom a good or satisfactory answer. It implies guilt or at least leads to the inference by some of guilt or of something being hidden.

The producer appeared, as arranged, at the regulator's office with an interviewer and a cameraman. All very friendly, initially, "to get your side of the story." The regulator's deputy and an assistant attorney general were present but off-camera—to signal or interrupt if the regulator got into forbidden territory, which could happen if examination findings were inadvertently (unlawfully) mentioned. The regulator was grilled for nearly two hours.

When the interviewer made a faux pas, which does and did happen, the producer said, "Let's shoot that again." When the regulator suggested rephrasing of an answer, the producer said, "No need. We won't be using that." (They didn't.)

The regulator was asked, "Were you in attendance at the March 17 meeting of the board of directors where (not when!) the board of directors refused to make any more cash advances to the builder and ended up foreclosing and taking over the partially completed property?"

The answer: "A federal regulator, representing the Federal Savings and Loan Insurance Corporation, and I were in attendance that morning." Here the regulator goofed. Wanting to keep answers succinct, his response was in two sentences, easily separated. "We were there just long enough for me to tell the board of directors that if they didn't find a merger partner by June 1 I would find one for them." That sentence was not aired! What was aired was that the two regulators were at the meeting. The goof: the regulator did not make it clear that foreclosure was presented and voted on in the afternoon session, when regulators were not present and had no knowledge of such action until after it had occurred.

Despite media sympathy for the builder, with considerable justification, the Supreme Court denied the builder's next appeal as being without merit. The regulator did and was doing his job without prejudice. Acting on advice from legal counsel he did not interfere with a civil suit being tried in court. He had removed the vice chairman of the board from office, whose signature was germane on a document. The chairman sold his stock and retreated to his original home in Canada. The regulator was advised he could not get him extradited. "His health is bad and he's old. Not worth the time and effort."

One officer of the association was sentenced to prison. He actually might have been, the regulator suspected but didn't have proof, the sacrificial goat for the actions of the board.

The notoriety of being seen on national television was not that enjoyable, but fellow state regulators understood and hailed him as a competent professional. He later told them, "In the future, if I know I'm to be interviewed on a delicate subject, I will have my own recorder active so I can have a comeback if ever I'm misquoted or something has been lifted out of context or twisted by a gratuitous editorial comment." Until one is burned or has reason to believe the interviewer is biased or even hostile, that tactic is not really necessary—and seldom as convenient as it would have been in the setting and circumstances described above.

Most reporters are talented and honest. Today, nine of ten are college graduates. When talking to a print reporter, however, remember that it is unlikely that person takes (real) shorthand. You will want to be deliberate, just as you are when on live television or being recorded for a radio broadcast.

One should start with the notion that media people are friends! Only if good reason exists should one be guarded with a reporter. However, there are a few who are lazy and will do the minimum to fulfill an assignment. Some are actually engaged in promoting their own agenda. Thus, one should be aware which editorial boards and publishers have reputations for being liberal or conservative if that is of any significance. This can influence a slant a reporter will take. Some reporters editorialize in news stories, especially on political issues. Yes, some are openly or subtly friendlier to either business entities or labor unions.

In every leadership role, but especially if you become politically active after developing your skills as a speaker, you will want to exercise more care in your choice of words. You may find that once in awhile even news disseminators may lift your words out of context and make a big show of trying to make you eat them. Publishers own their publications. They have every right to hire editors who are like-minded or at least can be counted on to reflect a liberal or a conservative view in editorials. Radio stations and television networks or independents have human owners who usually have strong ideas or philosophies. Most play it fairly straight, but it isn't difficult today for an astute reader, listener, or viewer to detect a liberal inclination in a majority of news outlets.

Back to your media relationships: If a reporter phrases a question in an awkward or to you an undesirable way, restate it and answer the question in such a manner that it is clear what you are answering. Keep answers short when possible, and do not indulge in jargon common only to your area of interest.

Reporters are not to be confused with commentators or entertainers on talk radio. Rush Limbaugh does not purport to be a reporter or to be unbiased. He is, by design, a rabble-rouser who stirs emotions and stimulates controversy and even thought. He has turned being interesting, admired, or hated, into a money machine that even some outstanding athletes could envy. Words that stimulate emotions are his stock in trade.

Television panelists on political programs often identify themselves or are identified as from the left or from the right. Even those not so identified are usually so outspoken and straightforward with their biases that a viewer doesn't have to work at figuring it out. There is no excuse for you to not know where a medium is coming from when you agree to an interview. You may get the fair and balanced assurance, but even then you must be alert to the possibility that an interviewer has an agenda and possibly a bias, however subtle.

The gift of gab can be quite important in a thirty-second interview on radio or for television. Even the quick quote for newspapers can enhance your image, your reputation, and possibly your career. When I was a city councilman I was once out-voted six to one. There was a pause as the mayor looked at me and asked, before striking the poised gavel, "Would you like to make it unanimous?"

My friends at the press table smiled, pens or pencils at the ready. Two of the three television cameras zoomed in on me. Two tapes were recording proceedings for later use on radio evening news programs.

"Six to one?" I queried with a smile. "Well, if you want to be wrong together I'll be right alone."

I've been wrong as often as most doers, but this time I was proven to be correct. The motion on the table was to put a proposal for levy for park development on the ballot at the forthcoming election. The media loved the spontaneity of the reply. Coverage was complete.

The background—and reason for my negative vote was this:

Two weeks earlier the mayor suggested council members check the pulse of the citizenry to see if a park bond issue would be met with favor. The mayor reported first and said everyone he talked to gave a favorable response. I had asked him earlier, in private, if he talked to anyone who didn't wear a suit and tie. I knew the circles in which he traveled. He had answered, "Well, the people I talked to are community leaders and they have a good feel for what's what."

I had sent fifty postcards explaining—neutrally—the proposition to barbers and beauticians, asking them to check the public pulse and give me a call in the next two weeks. Almost all of them did, some with generalities, a few with numerical counts. It appeared to me the vote would fail 60 to 40 or thereabouts. I knew we had not done a job of pre-selling usually necessary to get people to tax themselves, no matter how appealing the cause. The proposal was put on the ballot and went down, close to the figures my survey indicated. I volunteered to head a committee to sell the idea for a vote a year hence. That happened. It passed.

Your experiences will produce some good one-liners, but don't sweat it. We are not trying to be professional comedians. Some advisors say, "Just be yourself." The intent is nobly intended, but you and I know we have to be better tomorrow than we are today. I'm reminded of the words of a young man in a Sunday school class who came up with a show-stopper when the group was discussing the question presented by the leader, which was, "Which is most important, yesterday, today, or tomorrow?"

"Today" was leading when someone said, "Don hasn't said a word and class is about over. What do you think, Don?"

Don sat up straight, looked from left to right, and softly said, "I think our actions today should be based on our learning experiences of yesterday so tomorrow will be what we want it to be."

Wide eyes, pursed lips, nodding of heads, and silence of several seconds was followed by a smile from the leader. Then, "I think Don got us there just in time. We're adjourned." Too bad the media wasn't present so others could have heard those words.

Not all our utterances will be quotable, but those not comfortable in front of a TV camera or a print medium or radio interviewer must at least develop competence if they are or plan to become leaders. This is especially true if any part of such leadership is or could be related to politics. (And what isn't?) Anyone in politics or just in the public eye is fair game. Most people in politics are better human beings than their competitors paint them to be. In politics, defense is as important as offense, and sometimes more so. In this country we are experiencing more than enough public cynicism about government and those in government. My personal experience permits me to believe America and political leaders are not as bad as cartoonists (who have a lot of fun, I know) portray them. Exaggeration via caricature is often necessary to attract attention.

Knowing how to be succinct is a strong talent for a politician when others are being interviewed on TV with the same subject. Air time, public exposure, will be limited for each interviewee, and each participant is at the mercy of the TV staff member who will edit (reduce) the individual remarks. Again, an example serves to emphasize a point: When I was whip (that was number three in rank on the party's caucus leadership team, behind the majority or minority leader and the caucus chairperson) in the state senate, it was indicated I would be third of four interviewees, two from each party. With the camera rolling and the microphone being held inches before me, I heard the same question two predecessors had pontificated upon, in my opinion, too long. The same question was put to me: "Was this special legislative session called by the governor really necessary?"

"No."

The seasoned political reporter for a Seattle station appeared shocked. The opinion was no surprise to him but the unprecedented brevity obviously came as a genuine surprise.

He had to say, "Please—elaborate, Senator! Why not?"

"Our tinkering with the budget could have waited until the

regular session in January. This session was called for political purposes. There was no emergency."

Clean, simple, and the only response aired in its entirety. Unless one is engaged in an in-depth interview, emphasis should be limited to one point if possible and never (okay, never say never, so read that as "rarely") more than two.

Thinking on one's feet comes with experience, of course. Even professionals once in awhile have to say, "I wish I'd thought of that at the time instead in bed last night."

When you appear for a pre-scheduled speaking engagement at which the press is likely to be present and thus evidencing interest, you may wish to have printed copies of your remarks ready to be made available. The newspaper reporter will dig out and develop additional desired information through questioning. A radio reporter may record your remarks and be selective about lifting the most interesting portions. A TV reporter may or may not want a copy of your remarks. Your experience will tell you whether portions of such copies should be highlighted in advance. You may be interviewed or there may be a voice-over scene of the meeting. You may get extensive coverage or only a few seconds. Either way, it is likely to be a win/win situation for all.

Printed news stories (and programs), of course, are advantageous for scrapbooks and for use with resumes when one desires to make a career change. They also can be of value to those who seek speaking opportunities and advertise or do mailings in offering services, such as seminars, inspirational or technical talks, strategic planning weekends with boards of directors, or brainstorming (creative thinking) sessions for conventions, conferences, or individual corporate clients.

If your out-of-town talks and sessions are about moral issues or crusades or reforms, you might inquire or have your agent or publicist or a friend inquire of the appropriate editor(s) if there might be fodder for an editorial preview or follow-up. Copy on editorial pages can be reproduced and be just as valuable a tool as a news story. Self-promotion is a significant part of developing leadership qualities and making them known.

It is easy to ask/determine if your local news staffers prefer a finished copy of your remarks or just a fact sheet of highlights. Remember, it's been pointed out that news hounds are just people. They have egos, professional pride, and even professional jealousies. You might prepare or have prepared a news release that would get an A at the University of Missouri School of Journalism or at Medill School of Journalism at Northwestern University and still see a rewritten version in print in your local paper. Many reporters will feel obliged to put a professional touch to material provided. The lead and the conclusion are the most likely targets for a slight revision. You may consider it high praise, a hurried convenience, or even "Ho-hum, this looks okay," if ever the material you have submitted is printed verbatim. Do not be offended by intended improvement. You may learn that your regular news outlet prefers a series of one paragraph facts. They want to write the lead, the transitions or bridges, and the conclusion. So be it.

When you ask, you'll get varied answers, which you will learn to weigh against actual performance. Only your judgment can deal with contradictions.

In developing showmanship and media appeal, professional speakers may have a talent or booking agency. So—in addition to having help with their bookings and their scheduling, they may also enjoy assistance or even complete service in media relations. Advance publicity, scheduled interviews, and assured coverage by the media are not routine for speakers not on the professional circuit. Those making only occasional speaking appearances get to learn and do a lot of these things for themselves. While not routine in one's career efforts, neither is it difficult to get media coverage. Still, some competent show-boaters only get coverage in their in-house publications. Which is a good thing but not enough! One who is ambitious wants coverage in the local newspaper, radio, and television outlets. Maybe word of mouth references by audience members lead to additional appearances, but what's being missed? In marketing one's talents as a speaker, it is foolhardy to ignore or overlook the people who do not witness a performance. News broadcasts and news stories reach thousands or even millions. There are a lot of program chairpersons out there who need a program, a convention speaker, a consultant, a panelist for a conference, and you could be that person. Make someone look good for bringing you aboard and you'll get repeat business.

Corporate executives have some built-in advantages the freelancer has to pay to get. They (you?) can utilize the services of the firm's PR staff. Because the name of the organization is part of the identification of the speaker, the employer benefits. Public relations directors seek and encourage executives to display their platform skills. PR staffers can be called upon to do more than handle publicity. They often help with research, the development of material such as stage props and visual aids, and may even do some ghostwriting. If you are a business executive, help is as close as the telephone or just down the hall.

An alternate or additional source of help might be the firm's advertising agency. Some agencies have copy writers who also prepare news releases or even speech material and/or assistance for their clients.

Public speakers benefit by personal referrals, of course, but may also use direct mail or even paid advertising—or may become so accomplished or professionally engaged that there could be need to have an agent. A competitive edge belongs to those sufficiently enlightened as to how to benefit from what is broadly described as media relations.

Don't be shy, bashful, reluctant, or self-effacing. On the platform, when behind a microphone or in front of a camera, have awareness and appreciation of the job the media person is doing. Media coverage may occur because it's a slow news day and you got lucky. It is more likely that news coverage occurs because the sponsoring/host organization has a competent news or publicity chairperson. Leaving it to chance is not appropriate for a speaker desirous of maximum news coverage. The speaker should consider:

1. Advance stories
2. Utilization of local help
3. Pre-appearance interview(s)
4. A press conference (be careful and positive about the merits of such)
5. What the live coverage is going (or likely) to be
6. Distribution (or just availability) of printed material
7. Will this be local coverage, regional, state-wide, even national?

You may be accepting invitations to speak immediately (impromptu), later in the day, tomorrow, next week or next month, or even a year from now at the next annual convention of an organization. Usually your appearances will be scheduled weeks in advance, maybe months. Except for the unusual "Can you fill in?" there is opportunity for the story that you will be the featured speaker or a part of a larger program. It is at this point you determine the making of announcements to the media. The individual who extended the invitation can tell you the name and phone number of the organization's news or publicity chairperson and will suggest procedures or specific actions desirable. The topic will have been agreed upon. Who will be doing what? Respect for the person assigned is natural, of course, but one should evaluate the performance level likely. It may be necessary to offer to work together on pre-appearance publicity.

On the metropolitan daily and in the television newsroom there are personal egos under what may appear to be crusty or blasé exteriors. The business page editor is likely to judge a story on its merits, pure and simple. Personalized info from a trusted professional acquaintance, however, just might get a little more attention than material coming in "over the transom," as old-timers used to say.

Thus, those capable of and inclined to become acquainted with media reps will be winners for their efforts and interest in the other person. When you include a photo with the story of your forthcoming appearance, there's a chance it may be run. Space availability at the moment may be a determining factor, but odds are more favorable if the person making that decision knows and likes you. The status of the host organization could also be of consequence. That's the way it is! The same is true when a decision is being made about a pre-appearance interview. Odds vary. Local conditions, deadline schedules, and the time of your performance all enter into the decision-making. You and the news or publicity chairperson will arrange your availability with awareness of deadline schedules of media. Never beg or try to influence a medium by reminding someone your employer is an advertiser of consequence.

To state the obvious: Your message must be newsworthy! You may be presenting an insight to a known problem of general interest; a plan that will affect the lives of readers, listeners, and viewers; the revelation of significant hitherto un-reported facts; something that will affect our pocketbooks, our children, or our pets—well, if so, it probably will be considered newsworthy.

If a pre-appearance news conference is deemed by your host to be appropriate, they will have a location in mind. The local press club may be accessible or you may be in a meeting room at a hotel or in the boardroom of the host CEO. Just remember, you have to agree your message really merits bringing in busy pros.

Anticipating potential questions and advance preparation for such will enhance your ability to field what might be unexpected and/or difficult challenges. Truth will enhance your credibility if you are obliged to provide an answer not altogether favorable. Reporters do probe. They help an informed speaker show himself or herself to be an authority capable of getting a story across. The give and take at a press conference can make a speaker a local celebrity and thus enhance considerably the demand for appearances. Sure, you may err along the way, but you'll stretch your mind and even influence the behavior of others. That's what personal growth and leadership are all about.

Just as it is possible for a speaker to be unintentionally controversial, it is also possible a reporter or commentator may be biased (surprise!). Do not be a whiner or complainer if something negative happens to you, especially if in print or if you are on the air. You might be tempted to make the best speech you'll ever regret. Smile. When asked a question obviously designed maliciously to make you look bad, say something like, "I don't respond to garbage. Do you have a germane or pertinent question?"

Face this fact: If it bleeds it leads.

And there is always the human interest angle. There is routine reporting of the Eagle Scout award, top academic marks, society and church activities, the actions or inactions of governmental bodies. However, when you are seeking press coverage, remember: It had better be new or unusual to be considered newsworthy.

If you are in a television studio, the surroundings are determined by others. If you are hosting a television interviewer and a camera operator in your office or in facilities over which you have control or influence, you have determinations to be made and choices of trappings. Do you want a bare and orderly or a cluttered and busy desktop? Do you want to be in the lobby with the American flag in camera view, or maybe the picture of the board chairman on the wall? In any setting, you want to appear comfortable and confident, not intimidated or apprehensive. If an interview was unscheduled and you could be put into a defensive posture, do not recoil from a microphone being put before your mouth. Smile and gather your wits as necessary. Do not be concerned about a vacuum of silence, an admonition worth the repetition I realize it is getting. It is not your obligation to fill in blank time. Talk when you are ready and stop when you choose.

Consider news people to be friends. That, just as with everyone, improves the odds that they will be friends. You will, as you talk your way up your career ladder, be more comfortable and confident with the media as you polish your leadership skills. But—be aware you will always feel that extra rush of adrenalin when the TV camera is focused on you. You never want to lose the feeling of butterflies in your stomach. You simply want to get them into a favorable formation!

"When you face a television camera it is one-on-one contact. Each viewer is an individual, not part of a crowd. Talk to that camera as you do to one person."

ROBERT W. "BOB" SEVEY,
FORMER NEWS ANCHOR, KGMB-TV, HONOLULU

TEN

You Can Be in Control

*"But men must know, that in this theatre of man's life
it is reserved for God and angels to be lookers on."*

FRANCIS BACON

EVEN IN A LEADERSHIP ROLE one doesn't have to be an expert in parliamentary procedure to participate in live and lively proceedings. You will become as expert as you find necessary and/or desirable.

You will be inclined to keenly observe others serving as presiding officers. As a speaker you will be more aware of the performance of all involved in the presentation of a program.

As a presiding officer or even as a speaker you may face an individual or an audience not in tune with or even hostile to your position. Usually courtesy will prevail, but one can encounter a show-off desirous of illustrating his or her expertise. Rarely will one have to confront a heckler who—maybe for political reasons—tries to embarrass or challenge the person on the platform. Heckling ranges from the good-natured humorous approach to disagreement and possibly attempted abusiveness. If it is obvious there is honest disagreement and no likelihood of compromise or accommodation, you may find it pragmatic to agree to disagree amiably. You may then invite or urge the combatant and/or your audience to search further in a direction you suggest—and you will "agree to look further at the other point(s) of view expressed."

What about the heckler who is downright antagonistic, even verbally ugly? The one who will not be placated? That person may try to rattle you by attempting intimidation or, failing that, may become verbally abusive. You may encounter only a couple of such tormentors in your entire platform career, but it is well to be prepared mentally prepared for such a possibility. (You may run for an elective political office. Campaigns aren't as civil today as they were a few decades ago. Maybe history is cyclical. There was a time when even a duel was fought.)

Use put-downs only as a last resort. Usually, the audience will be on your side unless you have been overly-sarcastic or demeaning. A presiding officer should move to the lectern to curb or straighten out the offender. Do so when you preside. But—assume you are fending for yourself and remarks from the floor are unrestrained, to put it politely. A pit bull won't let go of the seat of your pants. Some in the audience are enjoying the verbal combat. Let's say you're in it and obviously on your own, under an unreasonable attack.

Start mildly and in good humor. For example, "Sir (or madam), you've made your point. I guess we should agree to disagree and move on, so if you will permit me to fulfill my role as the speaker of the moment, I will proceed." Smile and make the effort, assuming there will be no further interruption. If abuse continues, lower your voice gradually so the audience will tell the heckler to "Pipe down!"

Another technique is to restate in neutral tones an offensive question, possibly even tactfully paraphrasing. For example, "The question, as I understand it, is 'How come you flag-waving patriotic legislators are letting all those greasy, oil-rich foreigners dictate the economy of our country?' Sir (or madam), we aren't 'letting' anyone do any such thing. The facts of the matter are...."

This treatment tends to diffuse the question and permit rational discussion.

If attacked vociferously and mercilessly, stay calm. One rejoinder might be, "You obviously have had a course in debate. Apparently it did not include the art of listening." There are numerous possible responses to attacks. If you are likely to be engaged in controversy, you may wish to have a few ready. Senator Margaret Chase Smith, in an early stage of her career, listened with increasing impatience to the ranting of a young antagonist. Finally, exasperated and sensing the audience was also getting fed up with the exchange, she said, "You strike me as one with a lot of get up and go. You'd do all of us a favor if you would." The laughter of his peers left him subdued.

Another rejoinder is, "I recognize your right to freedom of speech, but I hope you don't think that freedom is a synonym for uncontrollable." Or, "Apparently some people approach problems with an open mouth." Or, "That's a gross idea, 144 times worse than the average." Or, "Some tell me your best quality is silence."

Remember, this is preparation for the unlikely, but it is satisfying to have a few shoot-'em-down rockets in one's arsenal. Here are a few I find entertaining:

"A lot of what you say is food for thought is coming across as baloney."

"A sage once observed, 'There are only three things that hiss: a goose, a snake, and a fool.' What have we here?"

Here's one used by a preacher who was an expert in human relations. I read it in "Just for Today," by James Keller of The Christophers, Inc.

Some noisy persons were disruptive during the service. The minister did not scold or manifest any sign of annoyance. "I am always reluctant," he said quietly, "to expose those who misbehave during services, because of an experience I had some years ago. A young man who sat in front of me was laughing and making grimaces. I was annoyed and rebuked him severely. Later I was told that I had made a grave mistake. The man I reproved had mental problems."

The noisemakers subsided.

If none of the above extricates you, turn to the presiding officer who has not been helpful. Ask, "Is this group organized enough to have a sergeant-at-arms? If not, perhaps I could donate to a fund to enable you to hire one."

The presiding officer should feel obliged to restore order and calm. Watching how the situation is handled could be of value if it is done well. If done poorly, remember this advice, given to me by my father: "Son, don't make fun of anyone. Everyone's good for something, even if only to serve as a horrible example."

Fortunately, most audience members are your friends. Those you haven't yet met are friends in the making. You probably will never have to use a put-down.

If you know in advance that you will face a hostile audience, say in a zoning debate about a proposed development in your neighborhood, you should know the technique of stacking the deck. You may assume those opposed to your position may be engaging in it. Chicago ward bosses exercise a "diamond" approach to create the impression of more support and strength than their numbers merit. The ethics may be questionable, but there is no defense against the practice other than a better offense. Visualize an auditorium or the chamber of a city hall. Neighbors of a like mind usually attend meetings in a cluster in the best available seats. Those planning to be vocal try to arrive early to get seats up front.

Be prepared to have at least four or more friends in your group. (Utilize numbers as appropriate.) Do not sit together! Position yourselves in a diamond shape, you in front, one (or some) at midpoint on each side, one (or two) at rear center. In each of the positions is at least one person who will speak to the issue.

When public discussion is in order, save your best remarks (presented by the most capable speaker) for the finale, the wrapup. Have one of your team speak early to influence the direction and flow of that which will follow. Then let the opposition show its hand. If it appears the opposition is gaining momentum, two of your team successively seek recognition from the chair. You may get some help from others like-minded, but in any case your forces have been coached in tactics and strategy. Timing is of significance! Try to have the first word and the last word—but not by the same participant. When your team senses victory or it's near decision time, your clean-up hitter (probably you) delivers the coup de grace, the assumed close.

We are assuming your cause is just and meritorious. However, those techniques are practiced by those not so noble, so do not let your people be victims.

Whether you are on the platform or at a neighborhood rally or leading a crusade, it is your leadership that will carry the day. This chapter is short but it should be more than sufficient to meet any negative situations you may face.

* * * * *

Now I am going to exercise editorial license and use personal experiences to offer what will be a couple of bonus points of interest to some but perhaps not for all readers.

By this time you have suspected or even detected that I qualify as an old-timer. There is an area in which I had a lot of fun (and some profit financially and career-wise). It is commonly called "brainstorming." Dale Carnegie instructors conduct the same activity as a "creative-thinking session." Either is correct. As a young man I read *Applied Imagination*, authored by Alex Osborne, a partner in the prestigious and internationally famous advertising agency of Batten, Barton, Durstine, and Osborne. That work earned for Osborne recognition as the Father of Brainstorming. A vice president of the Ethyl Corporation, Dr. Herbert True of Notre Dame, and I, then a vice president of the Chicago Jaycees, were three of the leading early practitioners. My most interesting performance as leader of a brainstorming session was in Washington, D.C., at a national convention where earlier I had the pleasure of sharing the speakers' platform with then Senator John F. Kennedy, Senator Margaret Chase Smith, and the president of a railroad. It didn't hurt my career when the *Chicago Daily News* ran a story on the front page of the second section that started with, "A young Chicago go-getter told them what for in Washington D. C. yesterday."

Rather than go into detail about brainstorming techniques here, I am going to refer those interested in learning more to conduct a search through Google or its equivalent. I did, just to see how much and what would be offered. There were seventeen headings and six or seven subtitles. One caught my eye because it was negative, indicating it was passé. However, by sheer and surprising coincidence, on the morning of June 3, 2008 I couldn't sleep and was reading the *New Yorker* magazine. On page 22 of the June 2 edition I read about a meeting in the conference room of a marketing firm. There was no conference table and a group of young New York businessmen were led in the discussion by a baby-faced 31-year-old who is working on his master's in international finance at Columbia. I quote: "...the meeting was conducted in a support-group-style circle of office chairs. The leader, Jeremy Goldberg, said, "It's ironic that we're meeting now, right in Hilary Clinton's back yard."

Mention was made of one idea contributor who is a candidate for a Ph. D. She, Bridget Guarasci, is writing her dissertation on Iraq politics. The subject being brainstormed was potential fundraising events on behalf of Barack Obama.

Reading this article convinced me that brainstorming is still alive and well and being practiced in a presidential campaign. Thus, it could be beneficial for the reader to do further research!

The second personal experience I will share has proved to be one of the most satisfying of my enjoyable life. Visualize a family of five, with two sons and one (middle) daughter, at the dinner table. We ate every meal together, but I did miss being with them more than did some "Leave it to Beaver" and "Father Knows Best" type fathers. My business travels took me out of state more than a few times a year. But—Friday nights I was home for the council meetings. The chairperson—that's one of the three kids, in turn—has developed an agenda, based on solicited and volunteered input from each participant. The chairpersons have been indoctrinated with how to preside at meetings, and know the orderliness of seeking recognition from the chair before speaking, how to make a motion, plus amending or substituting, which motions need a second, and how to conduct a vote. Just enough of Robert's Rules of Order to make it fun, not a chore or assignment!

The three all have advanced degrees, including one Ph. D. The daughter, with an MBA earned at age fifty with straight A's, is an executive with seventy-five employees reporting to her. She is an active Rotarian. Let's just say the boys are doing well. We have all been fortunate. The point is, all three, but especially the daughter, say that family council meetings gave confidence and courage to speak up at meetings in an orderly fashion.

If you have or will have a family, consider the merits of family council meetings. Orderliness, no raising of voices, the opportunity to present ideas or even resolve differences will enhance the talents, the lives, and the successes of you, your spouse, and your children. If this writer makes this contribution meaningful and beneficial to you, then that will be considered one of the most significant successes in his life.

* * * * *

To end on a positive note (always desirable!), let's conclude with a few generalities on which all members of this audience are likely to be agreed:

We each have unrealized capabilities.

We each would like to do something today that will make our tomorrows more enjoyable than they will be if we do nothing.

Beginning with family, friends, and associates with whom we have contact often, and with those with whom we have only occasional contact, we will be more interested in them as individuals, more conscious of their needs, wishes, and aspirations, and we will attempt to be more supportive and even more helpful. Honest!

"A truly elegant taste is generally accompanied with an excellence of heart."

HENRY FIELDING

Order Form

I would like to order additional copies of
Speak Up & Move Up!

Name: _____	
Mailing Address:_____	
E-mail Address: _____	
Quantity: _____ x $12.00 each *(10 or more books are $10.00 each)*	
Shipping and Handling $4.50 for WA state residents (includes sales tax) $3.50 per book for out of state residents	
Total Due:	

Send check or money order to:

R. H. Lewis
P. O. Box 5235
5815 Lacey Blvd.
Lacey, WA 98503

or send a request to:
email: rhbobtrooper@yahoo.com